The Heart Of The Matter

by

Rick Baldacci

Bloomington, IN  Milton Keynes, UK

authorHOUSE

AuthorHouse™
1663 Liberty Drive, Suite 200
Bloomington, IN 47403
www.authorhouse.com
Phone: 1-800-839-8640

AuthorHouse™ UK Ltd.
500 Avebury Boulevard
Central Milton Keynes, MK9 2BE
www.authorhouse.co.uk
Phone: 08001974150

First published by AuthorHouse 3/8/2006

ISBN: 1-4259-1236-2 (sc)

Library of Congress Control Number: 2005911388

Printed in the United States of America
Bloomington, Indiana

This book is printed on acid-free paper.

ACKNOWLEDGEMENTS

I could not have written this book without the encouragement of my dear friend Al Dawson. His wise counsel, insight and editing were invaluable to the birth and outcome of this whole project. I would also like to thank Edwin Pugh for his input, for the brotherhood we share, for the many conversations in front of his fireplace, and for introducing me to the beauty of some very special hideaways in the English countryside. Finally, I would like to express my sincere appreciation to Myran Walker, Jim Green, Nancy Short, Leona Jennings, Tim and Nina Sloan and Lori Finn for their helpful critiques and reassuring support.

INTRODUCTION

Day to day activities fill the pages of our lives; however, it is the poignant events that turn them.

These vivid emotionally charged moments encountered along the path of our personal history often waft in and out of our consciousness, triggered during a brief moment by a familiar aroma, a particular phrasing of words, a haunting melody, an extra squeeze in a tender hug, a savory meal or even an unusually colorful sunset.

Because these events hold such hallowed ground, they are easily resurrected. They come dressed in the same images of the past and rekindle many of the feelings last remembered. Some are warm comforting "reunions," welcomed home as one would welcome a friend. Others remain the sobering reminders they always were. A special few are as painfully sore as the day they happened. They are hard to relive, harder to forget, and are the hardest to share. Nevertheless, they are permanently inscribed on the walls of our souls and play a significant role in the sum of who we are.

Such is the journey of this book. I was challenged by a dear friend, whose trust and brotherhood I treasure, to share the inspirations for some of the poems I have written. I quickly realized that many of the inspirations emerged from a framework or fabric which wrapped itself around who I was and what made me want to write. Reflecting on those events and rediscovering the impact they had upon my life became essential to this goal.

I deliberately divided the book into three parts. Part One, Reflections, offers some of the early emotions, in the form of personal vignettes, as an insight into what role the intensity of those feelings played in the creative process. Part Two, Encouraging Hands, outlines the teaching and the guidance which enabled them to be valued, verbalized, and then captured through a variety of written styles. Part Three, Inspirations and Expression, the product of reflection and guidance, renders the outcome, what actually remained when the ink dried.

PART ONE:
__REFLECTIONS__

"Remembrance and reflections how allied;
what thin partitions sense and thought divide."

An Essay on Man. Epistle I.7.225
Alexander Pope. 1733-34

Seasons

"All changed, changed utterly:
A terrible beauty was born."
From Michael Robartes and the Dancer
Wm. Butler Yeats. 1916

It was an early spring morning in Virginia. I was five years old and sensing a newness in the air. Some of the leaves on the maple and oak trees had already started emerging in their light green colors. Mom had gotten me up early and as I was getting dressed, I was already thinking of playing with the toy cars at my neighbor's sandbox down the street. I was completely unaware that there was more change in the air than the changing of the seasons.

Mom said she had to run an errand which wouldn't take long. Within twenty five minutes we arrived at St. Bridget's Catholic School. We walked passed our church which lay perpendicular to the school and continued across an asphalt playground before we entered a gothic shaped doorway of a three story brick building. I could tell Mom was in her take charge mode as she grasped of my hand. She said she was looking for an office.

We stopped at a big black door with a translucent square glass inserted in the upper half. On it sparkled, in bright gold paint, the word, Principal. We went in and sat down. Soon a short plump nun came into the room, shook mom's hand and introduced herself as Mother Presentation. She then leaned over and shook my hand. She had a smell that was very distinct. It wasn't like perfume. It was more like the formaldehyde my brother used in the jars where he kept his black widow spider collection. My mom told me to sit still for a moment while she and Mother Presentation had a quick talk. The door was open to the room they went into and I could hear my mother insisting to Mother Presentation something about me but I couldn't quite hear the specifics. I kept hoping she would hurry up. I was ready to play with the kids down the street. I couldn't get my mind off that great sand box where we made terrific highways for our cars to travel. My impatience was soon rewarded.

Mom came out of the office with Mother Presentation but, instead of heading the way we came in, we began following her down a long hall with marble black and white tiles and oak doors spaced every twenty feet or so. I thought we were just taking another way out when we suddenly stopped at one of those black doors with cut square glass. Mother Presentation whispered that we must be quiet as she slowly turned the knob on the door. She interrupted the nun in the room, took me by the hand, and then led me in. The room was full of kids my age sitting in chairs formed in a circle. "This is Ricky Baldacci," she announced. "Can everyone say hello?" In unison all the kids in a sing song voice, shouted out, "Hello Ricky." Mother Presentation took me by the hand, led me to an empty chair, and asked me to sit down. Then she went back to where my mother waited and began having a talk with her and the other nun. Wait a minute, I thought. What's going on here? I'm not staying. Something is wrong. I don't want to be here. There has to be a mistake. Before I could voice any resistance however, my mother came over and, in a matter of fact voice, said it was time for me to start school...like all the other kids. She said, "I want you to be a big boy, listen to the teacher, Mother Theresa, and play nicely with the other kids." I could tell from my mother's face and the tone in her voice, the decision was made. She said she would be back at the end of the day to pick me up. With a quick hug she was out the door.

I tried to get up but Mother Presentation quickly blocked the way, grabbed a hold of my hand, and returned me to my seat. I remember trying to hold back my tears but they came rolling out of my eyes. I cried out, "Mom, come back. I don't want to stay here," hoping my distraught voice would bring her back. But I had seen the look on her face as she left the room. On hearing me yell, the other children broke out in laughter. I cried harder putting my face in my folded arms. It didn't take me long to stop because I knew it would be the only thing that would make them stop laughing, snickering, and pointing at me. Mother Theresa helped by starting to read a story and asking for quiet. I was grateful as this took the focus off me. I remembered thinking that the days of spending the morning playing in the sandbox down the street were over. I felt betrayed.

The seasons change slowly in Virginia as one gives way to another. This morning's change had been instantaneous. It was as if someone had simply turned off the lights, waited a brief moment, and then turned them on again. There was barely enough time to breathe, let alone adjust.

Yet with all the anger that was stirring in me, I knew my mother loved me more than life itself. It was always the trump card in my emotions and became the equalizer for that morning. As I started to take deeper breaths,

I resolved that if Mom wanted me in school, she must have a good reason. I didn't like how it happened but decided it was what it was. It was time to be a big boy.

Thus, one of my life's early lessons...adjusting to moments you can't control...got inscribed, and recorded.

It was an emotional day. It was a page turning day.

GUARDIAN OF THE FAMILY FLAME

"Oh, could you view the melody
of every grace
and music of her face,
You'd drop a tear;
Seeing more harmony
In her bright eye
Than now you hear."
From Lucasta. Orpheus to Beasts.
Richard Lovelace. 1649

From first grade through the eighth, there was a rhythm to living. Monday through Friday it was rise and shine at six thirty; don my school uniform made up of navy blue pants, white shirt, blue bow tie, and navy blue sweater...and then follow my nose. Mom usually had "brown and serve" rolls waiting in the kitchen on which we put butter and ham. I always thought it was the greatest smell in the world to wake up to. The rolls were often accompanied by scrambled eggs, sausage patties or links and applesauce, or pancakes with maple syrup.

Our house was heated by an oil furnace. There was a large metal grate on the floor in the hallway which led to our bedrooms, and in the morning you had to be careful how you stepped on it with bare feet. You could get a "waffle burn" without realizing what you had done. The furnace was the only source of heat in the house and often broke down. On those cold mornings, Mom would close the swinging doors to the kitchen, and let the heat from the stove warm the room. I would grab my clothes, run to the kitchen and dress there. Mom was always cheery in the morning, always giving me a big hug and kiss. It was the best of all worlds: good smells, savory food, warm room, engaging conversation, and unconditional love.

My mother always had a way of making the best of a bad situation. It was one of her greatest strengths. From the big things to the small, she knew how to focus on the good and disarm the bad. When I came home with mud all over me and my clothes, her first greeting at seeing me at the back door was, "It looks like you had a great day!" She always wanted to hear about "my adventures". Then she would say, "Now why don't you take off your dirty clothes there and go in and wash up". It didn't mean we wouldn't have a "talk" later but it left open a special communication channel. I felt free to want to share with her my joy without fearing it would be squashed before opening my mouth. The impact of this lesson continues to echo in my thinking. Its wisdom frequently moves me to tears.

Mom normally drove me to school; however, within a few weeks she had to go back to work to help my father bring in much needed extra money. From then on I rode the school bus. I was the antithesis of a "latch key child". Yes, I got home before Mom and Dad returned but I never stayed inside. The neighborhood was filled with kids and our afternoons were spent playing sports in the back yards behind our houses. Baseball, football, and basketball were always at the top of the list. Mom also allowed me to ride my bike several blocks to the local drug store. I couldn't take the main road as there was too much traffic. I had to wind my way through our development on the back roads to get there. It was a taste of independence and responsibility for a third grader that, in today's world, would be unthinkable. But "back then" it was a different world. What a treat it was after a game to hop on my bike, ride in convoy with my buddies to the Rexall Drug Store, buy a pack of baseball cards, and slurp down a cherry coke!

Yet, with privileges came rules and absolutes. I had to be home when Mom came home. Absolutely no game in any yard, however close in score, or trading any set of baseball cards could preempt being home for supper time. I knew this was Mom's "line in the sand." Cross it and risk losing not only Mom's flexible attitude but worse…her trust. Her countenance would noticeably change and her voice would grow softer in tone. My brother and I used to say that disappointing Mom was the hardest thing to endure. She was our biggest cheerleader, advocate, appellate judge, and relief pitcher. When Dad was coming down on us, Mom was "in there" looking for loopholes in the length and degree of discipline, reminding him of our better qualities and seeking to save the day. Not having Mom feeling her best about you was tantamount to disaster. It became our greatest motivation to be obedient.

Half of the time, Saturdays became a continuation of afternoon games played during the week. Yet other times it was a day to play army in the woods across the street. We would choose up teams, usually two to three on a side. Then one team would disappear into the woods as the other team would start their "search and destroy" mission. Clad in army helmets, ammo belts, camouflage clothing, black smudged faces, plastic machine guns and Colt.45 revolvers, we relived our own "Operation Overlord" over and over again. Mom was the mess hall. She would have snacks waiting for both teams as we took time out mid-afternoon for R&R. "The guys" loved coming to our house. Yes, they gorged themselves on her chocolate chip cookies covered with powdered sugar but they also devoured the love that came so naturally from her. Watching their reaction only confirmed in me what a gift I had been given.

Sunday's were always "church days." We would go to mass at St. Bridget's Church and then keep our "good clothes" on for Sunday lunch.

Church was always followed by a number of joyous options: visiting Big Momma and Big Daddy (grandparents), feeding the ducks bread crumbs at Byrd Park with loaves of bread bought at the local grocery, riding flattened cardboard boxes down the steep grassy hills of a city reservoir near the Carillon and "Nickel" Bridge, eating fried chicken at "Chicken in the Rough," smelling the sweet aroma of vanilla being bottled at Sauer's Factory at Boulevard and Broad.

On Sunday there was no democracy in our family. Dad categorically stated that Sunday was Mom's day. We could express our desires but it was Mom who always got the deciding vote. The option my mother chose most often was visiting one of her many sisters. She had six sisters and four brothers. My mother was singer, who in her late teens, sang with an orchestra. She also made singing cigarette commercials for national radio distribution in New York City. In addition, she teamed up with two of her sisters, Ann Bryan and Lou Chancey to perform all over Virginia as the "Mac" Sisters. Mom couldn't wait to get to one of their houses and insist we all gather around the piano. Once the singing began, usually with a rousing rendition of "Alexander's Ragtime Band" or "Sweet Georgia Brown", I knew it would be hours before we would leave. I used to think it was a lucky thing each of her sisters had kids my age. Ann had four daughters and Lou had two daughters and a son. We became fast friends. Formally we were first cousins but over time we became so much more.

It didn't take long for me to hope Mom would choose the "sisters option." I grew to love listening to the fantastic vocal harmonies and the rhythmic sounds emanating from the piano. Even more I enjoyed the moments when they insisted all of us sing with them. These musical gatherings became the strongest bonding events I knew as a child. There was such a feeling of acceptance that it redefined my understanding of the word....family.

And in those moments when we were all hugging each other because the last song moved us to complete exultation, I remember staring at my mother, marveling at the way her spirit brought the best out in people. Her insistence on spending time with her sisters and gathering families opened doors on so many levels and laid the foundations for many family traditions.

Marguerite Francis McDonough Baldacci, "Mom", was an amazing woman, mother and "guardian of the family flame". The grace, hospitality and encouragement she extended to everyone who crossed her path were a breath of fresh air, a cool comforting moment of shade, on a hot sweltering day.

APPELLATION MOUNTAINS

Somewhere, with all these clouds, and all this air,
there must be a rare name, somewhere...
How do you like "Cloud-Cuckoo-Land"?
From The Birds by Aristophanes.

I hated the first day of any school year. I knew the unavoidable drill. Each teacher would call roll enunciating each student's full name. My name consistently brought the class to laughter. "Henry Ricardo Baldacci"...the nun would slowly utter with what seemed a smirk on her face. I always had my eyes closed, and mentally whispered a prayer that somehow everyone in the class would be so distracted that it would not be heard. That never happened. There was always an immediate eruption of laughter followed by mocking shouts of "Henry Ricardo"! Then came the inevitable pushes on the back and pokes in the side from the guys sitting around me. It was a ten minute first day hazing I had to endure every year.

It could have been worse. Mom wanted to name me Ricky Ricardo because, when I was born, she was watching *I love Lucy*, the favorite sitcom of the day, and she adored the characters. My uncle Henry, the husband of Momma's favorite sister Anne, just happened to visit before my Mom made it official. So touched by his kindness, she decided to give him top billing. I guess it could have been worse. She might have, in a moment of frivolity, named me Fred Mertz Baldacci, or Fred Henry. Looking back, the perturbations were too overwhelming. It is sufficient to say I was dubbed and learned to live with Henry Ricardo. Momma never gave up on her original plan, however she always, with an endearing voice, called me Ricky Ricardo.

As much as I used to wonder about my mother's "sanity" when naming me, she actually got the last laugh. After receiving my undergraduate degree in 1970, my first foray into corporate America came in 1973 as a Personnel Supervisor, working for a young smoke detector manufacturing company in Lakewood, Colorado. Always wanting to avoid discussions about my name, I made sure my business card read "H.R. Baldacci" and quickly identified myself as Rick. By the time I moved to my second job, as a Personnel Manager, the corporate world decided that the designation "Personnel Department" conjured up too many negative connotations of the past and also wasn't forward thinking enough for the ever changing dynamic work environment. They decided to break with the past and infuse new life into the profession with a vibrant, thought provoking moniker "Human Resources." I don't think the irony of the name struck me until one day, one member of my staff asked me, "Don't you find it ironic that your name is HR Baldacci?" Then in an instant the realization hit me. It was one of those moments that made you pause and think about the coincidences of life. A tape in my mind quickly played out the whole naming saga which left me staring off in the distance. I remember the employee persisting, "Well, don't you?" "You don't know the half of it," I said with a chuckle as I headed off to my office.

As I made my way, the famous line Ricky Ricardo (as played by Desi Arnez) used to use when he was frustrated with Lucy popped into my mind. In his infectious Cuban accent he would say, "Lucy, you got some 'splaining' to do!" My mother's face flashed across my thoughts and I softly grinned. To myself I whispered, "Momma, if you can hear me 'from up there'...It's about my name. This time it's not you who has some 'splaining' to do; rather, this time it is I.

My mother and I always seemed to have our best conversations in the kitchen. She wisely knew that certain favorite foods had "medicinal qualities," and could lighten a heavy heart. The intoxication of those wonderful aromas would set my tongue to wagging. Whatever was on my heart came pouring out, much to her delight. She listened intently, never allowing anything to distract her. She was a female Socrates. She would ask questions and often replied to my answers with another question. She truly wanted to know exactly what the issue was and how I felt about it. Even if I was "way off base" in my thinking, she would never belittle any of my thoughts, disappointments or fears. She carefully and skillfully utilized her gifts of dialogue, compassionate questioning, and undivided attention to gently nudge me to reconsider whatever seemed discordant with my position. I wish I could express the powerful influence these gifts had on my life. Perhaps the greatest testimony is to acknowledge the profession through which I have been fortunately able to support a family and sustain a career: interviewer and personal coach.

Mom made the kitchen a sanctuary. Everything there was safe. It was a place I could let down my guard and put up my feet. She would laugh at my jokes, howl at my school stories, and beg for more. Best of all, she was tight-lipped. I never had to worry about anything I said going further, especially to Dad. He was a good father but had little time for long conversations. He was more the "here's what you do" or "you shouldn't let stuff like that bother you" and "let's move on" kind of person.

Growing up I gradually realized that you need both types. Some days you want a "drive through restaurant" type of conversation, other days you want to go in and sit down.

Regrettably, my mother passed away a few years before this whole evolving reality on my name arose. It would have been the subject of a great kitchen table "sit-down" meal together. She would have laughed, and rejoiced at being vindicated. I would have savored every moment of it.

PALPITATIONS

"Love is…born with the pleasure of looking at each other,
it is fed with the necessity of seeing each other,
it is concluded with the impossibility of separation."
From Amor
Jose Marti.1881

Her name was Susan. It was fourth grade. She represented a whole set of new feelings. She had brown hair, blue eyes, and a smile that struck every prepubescent gene inside of me. I tried to sit next to her in class, get behind her in line to the cafeteria, and during recess run through the circle of girls she stood in pretending to be focused on a football keep away game. All of this was a desperate attempt to get her to notice me. I wasn't sure why I needed to have her attention but something inside me kept urging me forward. These were new feelings, strong and confusing, while humorously debilitating physically.

I put all my effort into becoming an athlete. It is what earned you status with the "in-crowd" on the play yard. I wasn't the most talented but I knew I was considered "a player" by the guys as I was picked early when two captains were choosing teams from the group of guys standing in front of them. To me, that designation was worth its weight in gold and proved to be a ferocious motivator.

I spent endless hours playing pick up games with kids in the neighborhood. When they were not available, I begged my brother to throw a ball with me. A neighbor from across the street, eight years older than me, put up a basketball hoop. We played "around the world" and "horse" incessantly.

When no one was available to play, I created my own version of a baseball game. I would throw a hard rubber ball against our back stoop. If it hit the flat part it would come back to me as a ground ball. I would scoop it up and throw another quick toss at the step to make sure it would careen off in such a way as to come at me like the throw from an infielder. I would pretend to catch it like the first baseman. If by chance it would hit the corner of the step, it would come to me as a fly ball. If the ball passed by me on the ground it was a single, double or triple. If it went far over my head, it was a home run. Being the pitcher for both mine and the opposing team, I would pitch to the lineups of any team as they played my favorite team, the New York Yankees. I threw as hard as I could and let how the ball hit the steps be the determining factor.

By the time I reached fourth grade, with untold hours of practice, I could throw a football twenty yards on target to a running wide receiver, sink a jump shot from anywhere around the key, and play baseball with some fairly strong all around skills.

However, around Susan, I stumbled over my own feet, tripped over "fresh air," and ran into doors. It was as if every athletic gene in my body took the day off. Moreover, every word that came out of my mouth seemed from the Czech Republic or Japan. It was if someone had anesthetized my tongue. Lamentably, my brain was not far behind either. If there was an opportunity to say something wrong at just the right time, it became inevitable. I was sure I set new standards for imbecilic behavior. Nevertheless, the rising magma of these new emotions kept picking me up, dusting me off, bandaging my heart, and sending me back into the ring. I took an emotional pounding in fourth grade. Yet, the special feeling of being near her and the joy of catching her smiling at me always left me ready for more.

As quickly as the flood of these feelings came, so too did the reality of how to deal with them. There was an unwritten play yard, fourth grade code about all this: Don't be caught with those kinds of thoughts! Guys, even best friends, with this kind of information could be merciless in their teasing. Emotions and subtleties had to be kept inside and unspoken. Any contact or interaction with a girl had to look spontaneous and meaningless. Rules were rules...guys were guys...and the price to be paid for violating this unwritten compact was intimidating. It certainly was enough to keep me in line, at least for the fourth grade.

With Susan I was only left to secretly fantasize about where a year's worth of quick hellos, short class interactions, occasional lengthy stares and tender smiles during class, might have led. But in a much bigger way, I had opened the door to the world of "puppy love," and had fallen prey to the addicting aroma of its sweetness. As every boy learns, it is delightfully debilitating.

WINGS

If fourth grade was a time of prepubescent discovery, seventh grade became a rite of passage; a time to stretch one's wings. What was codified and set in stone in fourth grade, with regard to rules of engagement with girls, methodically crumbled away over the next two years. The new rules not only allowed contact with girls, they encouraged it. In fact, it became as much a status symbol as athletic prowess. That was strange I thought, yet somehow it made good sense. I had already noticed a cute girl named Katrina sitting two rows over who had stared at me in class. Every day became a new awakening not only to the opposite sex but also to an unfolding world.

In addition to this new social agenda, seventh grade brought many other "revelations." Alan Shepard became the first American astronaut to fly in space. Our teacher, Mother Dominic, brought a television into our class. That too was a first. She announced that there was going to be an attempt to send an American into space and hoped we could be witnesses to this moment in history. I hadn't heard anything about any of this and remember being overwhelmed by the enormity of it all. Where had I been when this was being scheduled for broadcast? When had President Kennedy announced this, I wondered? When had we started an astronaut program? While one question after another came to me, the television was turned on. My eyes locked onto the CBS broadcaster. On the screen came a close-up picture of Alan Shepard getting out of a NASA van and carrying his portable air conditioner as he walked toward the Redstone rocket which would carry him into space. Images of "Captain Midnight" flashed into my brain. I chuckled to myself wondering if he had a decoder ring. But as quickly as those images ran through my consciousness, the reality of what was happening set in as he climbed into his space capsule which he had named Freedom 7. The gantry pulled back and the countdown continued. There were delays in the countdown which only heightened the anxiety that everyone in my class was feeling. Eventually, what seemed like was not going to happen, happened.

As the countdown reached one minute…then thirty seconds…then ten, nine, eight, seven, six, five…involuntarily those of us near the back of the room stood up straining to get a better view…four, three, two, one….liftoff. Alan Shepard communicated "The clock is started." As we watched the rocket thunderously clear the launch pad, it slowly climbed into the blue sky over Cape Canaveral. All eyes were glued on the white trail of smoke his Mercury capsule left as it sped "down range" on its fifteen minute suborbital flight. "Everything is A-OK," shouted Alan Shepard to capsule communicator Gus Grissom. The classroom broke out into riotous applause! It wasn't long before his capsule splashed down in the Atlantic under the canopy of a huge parachute. The rescue helicopter circled overhead and pulled him up out of his raft with a sling harness. From there he was carried to a nearby aircraft carrier. I was awe struck, simply captivated. New emotions welled up inside. Roy Rogers, the Cisco Kid, and Davy Crockett suddenly didn't look the same. I had found a new, real life, bona fide hero. Alan Shepard will never know what he did for me that day, May 5, 1961. In many ways he pulled back the clouds and gave me my first real look at the stars. He made me want to look over the horizon.

He launched in my heart a realization that there was so much more to learn than the little microcosm I had constructed. I remember running home from the bus stop that day and eagerly looking for the Richmond Times Dispatch, the Richmond News Leader, and our Life magazine. For the first time reading took on new meaning and became its own new kind of exploration. Words such as, "mission control," "telemetry," "yaw," "pitch," "roll," "attitude," "angle of attack," "heat shield" and others leapt into my vocabulary. I started a set of "space program scrapbooks" and found myself leaving one world and entering another. With Alan Shepard and the other Mercury astronauts, Gus Grissom, John Glenn, Scott Carpenter, Deke Slayton, Wally Shirra, and Gordon Cooper, the space program was heading into orbit.

The times were changing and so were the rules. Emotionally and intellectually, I recognized I was still back at Kitty Hawk; however, for the first time I knew I eagerly wanted to explore what it felt like to leave the ground.

GIFTEDNESS

"Patience is a necessary ingredient of genius."
From the Young Duke
Benjamin Disraeli. 1831

It was a typical Virginia summer afternoon. The temperature was well into the nineties and the humidity wasn't far behind it. Sitting on the back porch of our row house in the "Fan District" of Richmond, my brother and I were talking about inane things to pass the time and take our minds off the heat. Suddenly his eyes grew fixed on something over my shoulder. "Look at that," he said pointing to some telephone lines that ran parallel to our street. "I don't see anything," I responded, scouring the lines not knowing what he had spotted. He got next to me, put his left hand on my shoulder and had me gaze down the length of his right arm. "Look just past that pole and then you will see a little bird." "Oh yeah, I see it!" I exclaimed. "What is it?" "It's a parakeet," he said emphatically. "Don't you see the green and blue feathers on him and the tuff on his head?" As soon as he said those words, I did see it. "Wow! What is he doing up there?" "He probably got out of his cage, or someone just didn't want him and let him go. He won't live long in the wild." What happened next will live in my memory forever. "Keep your eye on him. I'll be right back. I've got an idea," my brother said as he ran into the house. As quickly as he had gone he was back with a tiny bell in his hand. "Get in the house. You can watch through the back window," he snapped as his eyes focused on the parakeet which hadn't moved. I knew my brother's tone of voice and jumped to his command. I dashed into the house and peered through a tiny slit in the Venetian blinds. My brother sat quietly on the back porch with his eyes intently focused on the parakeet. Then he began ringing the bell with a vibrant deliberate rhythm. I could hear the ting-a-ling-a-ling, ting-a-ling-a-ling coming from the bell and wondered what in the world was he thinking. My brother's head was still. The only movement coming from him was his hand. Minutes slowly passed by. Nothing happened. More and more time passed. He had been at this almost an hour. I wanted to yell out, "Come on Teddy, let's go do something," but I knew better. You didn't mess with him when he was this intent. That was too big of a price to pay later on.

Just as I was about to leave to go do something by myself, the parakeet moved. He flew from the telephone line to a corner of our roof. Instantly I understood my brother's idea. The bell! It was the bell that was luring him closer! The parakeet must have had a bell in his cage and recognized the sound! Brilliant, simply brilliant, I thought. What made Teddy think of that? Now my mind raced. Okay, you can get the parakeet to respond to the bell but how in the world will you catch him? Now my attention grew as intent as my brother's trance-like state. It reminded me of how a lioness stares at her prey, muscles tensed and yet perfectly still. Ting-a-ling-a-ling, ting-a-ling-a-ling, he steadily continued the ringing of the bell. I could see the parakeet turning his head with every ring of my brother's hand. He examined every part of my brother over and over. Ting-a-ling-a-ling! Calmly and persistently my brother kept up his rhythm. Minutes passed. Then the parakeet flew and landed on the back porch railing just a few feet from where my brother sat. I was stunned by my brother's nerves of steel. Methodically, as if he were in slow motion, he turned toward the parakeet and gently rang the bell with a slower pace. In addition, he put his left fist on the railing a few feet from the bird, extending the left index finger of his left hand as if pointing. At first the parakeet hopped back, ruffling his wings. I thought, "oh no, he's lost him" but sighed a breath of relief when the parakeet settled down and continued to rapidly turn his head at the sound of the bell.

My brother is persistent, calculatingly so. For what seemed like another half hour, he rhythmically shook the bell. Finally, the parakeet inched closer to his finger and then confidently hopped up on it! My heart was pounding as my brother slowly got up and started a deliberate pace toward the back door. I could hear him softly ringing the bell for the parakeet as he opened the back screen door and walked in, steady handed. As the door closed, I whispered, "Unbelievable, you are unbelievable!" My brother flashed back his effervescent victory smile and humbly said, "Thanks."

To the victor came the spoils. He named him "Tony." We bought a wire cage and stand and proudly displayed him in our living room. After all, this parakeet came with "an amazing story." Our whole family enjoyed him, his love of bells, mirrors, and his amazing ability to mimic in the accented voices he heard for another ten years!

My brother has always had the gift of being at the right place at the right time, a gift he proved over and over as we grew up. His exploits are legendary. As a kid he brought home every animal, arachnid, and reptile from the woods and creeks nearby: all kinds of venomous and non-venomous snakes, gigantic snapping turtles, flying squirrels, ducks, salamanders, opossum, rabbits, spiders, pigeons, doves, chipmunks…and the list goes on and on.

How he found them, caught them, and carted them home, never ceased to leave me amazed.

However, this incident with Tony became the launching point for a mystique and an aura which reached "super hero" proportions. My feelings for him soared. He was certainly the punctuation point of my childhood. He evoked from me more emotion than I thought possible. It was difficult then to put into words the love I had for him. Just being around his giftedness was a privilege and a daily adventure in wonderland.

TATTOOS

Some pages are so painful, that when they turn, they take your breath away. You remember breathing in but you don't remember breathing out. They are indelible moments, much like tattoos in your memory that don't fade away, not even when you close your eyes and try to erase them. They are stingingly vivid and often dredge up many of the awful feelings that accompanied them. They are always sobering. They are boxed up, put in the trunk of your soul, and carried through life. They are heavy when carried alone and lighter when they are shared.

I thought I would do some unpacking today.

There was a loud "boom"; the ground shook, and then there was a scream...more like a shriek. "Ricky!" my mother screamed. I was playing in the next door neighbor's walkout basement. I knew my mother's angry voice but it wasn't anger I heard. This one was much louder and had a tone of terror and panic in it. It came from our front yard. It rang out again and again. I ran as if her scream had injected adrenalin into my veins. As I came into the front yard, Mom came running and grabbed me. She lifted me up and hugged me as if I had gone away somewhere and just returned. I felt like a rag doll and she spun me around hugging and kissing me saying "Thank you Lord." When she stopped, I finally caught a glimpse over her shoulder of what had happened. A huge dump truck had overturned in our front yard and rested upside down on its back. It had been full of gravel which now had spilled all over our yard. The dust that had been kicked up created its own weather system. My first thoughts were amazement. The truck had not rolled into our yard but hit our ditch with its front bumper. This had catapulted the backend straight up and then over on its back. It was as if the truck had tried to do a somersault and just failed to follow through. Then the reality of why Mom was sobbing with relief came to me. My friends and I had just been playing on that very spot. We had, by a quirk of coincidence, gone to their house to get something from their basement. From the size of the truck and the displacement of the gravel, there was no doubt that anyone in the front yard would have been in the wrong place at the right time. I don't think previously I had ever thought about dying. That day, however, the possibility crept into my mind for the first time, and the sound it made, as it reached my soul, was deafening.

It was early Sunday morning. My brother was spending the night with a neighbor across the street and I was alone in the bedroom we shared. Mom had just gotten up and was about to get out of bed to start fixing breakfast. Dad, generally the early riser, was walking toward the front door in his tee-shirt and boxers to get the morning paper. Suddenly, the sound of "Pop! Pop!...Pop! Pop! Pop!" came from the front yard of our next door neighbor. Dad ran to the window and peered out. Then there were more "Pops." I heard Dad say, "Who is shooting off fireworks this early?" Then with a stern voice he snapped, "O my God! Stay in the house." He raced to get his bathrobe and then ran out of the front door. I flew to the living room window in curiosity. We saw Dad was standing over two people who were lying in the yard next door, one close to the house, one farther out. Dad came running back to our front door when Mom met him. He said in a hurried voice, "Call the police. Tell them there has been a shooting." He returned to the two people lying still on their front lawn. Within minutes more neighbors had come to the scene, as did the police. An ambulance raced up, loaded the body farthest from the house and sped off. The police had put a sheet over the body closest to the house. Dad spent a long time talking with one of the officers. Newspaper photographers showed up and began taking pictures. Then a man in a dark suit arrived and started examining the person under the sheet. Soon a hearse arrived and the body was put into the vehicle.

Wait a minute, I thought! Where are Betty and Barbara? Betty and Barbara were the two young girls who lived next door. We were best buddies. Betty was one year older than me. Barbara was one year younger. We were forever building forts in our back yard, playing hide and seek, eating meals together, and going to the Saturday afternoon matinees at our local theater. Our moms would get together on Saturday nights to watch the Lawrence Welk Show on television. Betty was a good dancer and taught me how to do the polka. We would entertain our parents by dancing as the Lawrence Welk band played one lively tune after another. Betty had a zest for life as she was always pushing the limits of everything she did. If I needed a shot of adrenalin, Betty was there to offer it. Some days she was fun; others she was exhausting. Barbara was the introvert, the opposite of her sassy, brassy sister. She had a sweetness and genuineness about her that made her more fun to be with than many of my guy friends. I could relax around her and never worry about her motives. The two sisters were an interesting contrast and cemented many of the early distinctions I made about young women.

After what seemed two hours, Dad slowly made his way back to our house, shaking his head in disbelief. He told us that Betty and Barbara's father had been waiting for their mother, his estranged wife, and her boyfriend to come home. She worked the graveyard shift at a local cigarette factory and he knew what time to expect them. As she got out of the car and walked toward the house, he jumped out of his car which he had inconspicuously parked, brandishing a pistol and followed her. In a fit of rage, he shot her in the back. She recoiled and fell face down near her front steps. He then turned the gun toward the boyfriend who was still near his car and fired a shot. Miraculously, he missed. As the terrified boyfriend jumped into his car and sped off, the husband fired several more shots all of which missed their target. The husband then went to his car reloaded his pistol and with a deliberate pace, walked back to where his wife lay on the ground. He took his foot and kicked her over on her back. Looking down at her, he raised his gun, aimed at her chest, and fired. Bam! Bam! Bam! Bam! Bam! She convulsed with each shot. He left one round in the chamber. Then he sat down near her, held the gun with both hands, aimed at his chest, and squeezed the trigger. Bam! The last shot rang out. When Dad arrived seconds later, he could see that the wife was dead. The husband, lying flat on his back, was moaning and bleeding badly.

As Dad somberly related what he had seen and discovered, he kept pausing with deep sighs trying to come to grips with the macabre event which had unfolded in front of his eyes. Mom sat beside him, comforting him with one arm around his shoulders and the other holding his hand.

My thoughts leapt to Betty and Barbara. What must they be thinking? Were they huddled in their house crying? Did they hear the gun being fired? Is anyone taking care of them? What must they be feeling…losing a mother and possibly a father in a moment of madness? Where would they go to live? What happens when your parents die? This was new ground and I wasn't used to the shroud of numbness that moved in on my psyche. As sad as I was for them, I couldn't stop thinking about this new emerging reality. What would I do if both of my parents were to be taken suddenly? My mind started racing through the options. I wondered which of my relatives would take us into their home. Would my brother and I be allowed to stay together or would we be separated? Who would decide all of this? I quickly thought of my father and what must be flashing through his mind.

My dad's father died of pneumonia when Dad was in his early twenties. My dad was the oldest of eight siblings. When the funeral was over, his mother looked at him and said, "Okay, you are the Dad now. What do we do?" For my dad, that was a "page turning day," a "tattoo" he dealt with every day. It was one of those hard lessons where life hauled off and slapped him in the face. He didn't have time to prepare. It happened in one traumatic instant, and then he was left to deal with it in the best way he could. It became one of the hallmarks of his testimony on how to face life one day at a time.

Every chance he could, he would build in us resiliency, adaptability, and a survival mentality to overcome the worst of "storms." He knew they would come. On that Sunday morning, sitting in the living room of our house on 6916 Horsepen Road, he seized the moment with me. In his "you need to hear this voice," he said, "Never take any day for granted. Count your blessings. Be strong. Other people may need to rely on you."

I couldn't imagine how Barbara and Betty were being told that message, much less their reaction. Words began welling up in my soul, begging to be written. I should have put them down and hand delivered them; however, I was too paralyzed worrying about saying the wrong thing. I just put them in the box of my soul. They are still there.

I can't imagine the pain you must feel. I loved your mother. She was always so kind to me. I can't bear the thought of her being gone forever. What must you be feeling? If you need to talk or even cry, I built a fort in the back yard. Whenever you want, I will meet you there. I am so sorry that this happened. It scares me to think of what lies ahead for me.

Betty and Barbara's father survived his attempted suicide. He was charged with first degree murder and attempted first degree murder. He was convicted and sentenced to over 40 years in prison. Betty and Barbara went to live with a relative and I never saw them again.

There are some things you can talk about with your parents and others you are almost afraid to ask because you don't want to know the answer. I decided that resolving the question of where I would go had too many emotional pitfalls. Losing two good friends was hard enough to deal with. I opted for the "Scarlett O'Hara" theory of management and "left it for another day."

Their formal names were William Vincent McDonough and Blanche Haines. We called them "Big Daddy" and "Big Momma." They were my mother's father and mother. Big Daddy was a policeman; Big Momma was a piano teacher. They raised eleven children, seven daughters and four sons. It was a traditional Irish Catholic Family. We regularly visited them after church in the "Churchill" area of Richmond when I was in grade school and in south Richmond where they moved when I attended high school. Big Daddy had a vintage Harley Davidson motorcycle in a shed behind his house which always caught my brother's and my interest. We would go to see it while Mom and Dad were paying their respects.

Big Momma would always greet us with "Hi, darling. Come here and give me some sugar." She had a twenty inch waist when she got married but, after eleven children, looked more like "Mammy" in Gone with the Wind. Big Daddy was tall and thin, mostly stoic, never saying much in a crowd. He had received a serious head injury while working on the police force and had to have a plate put in his head. Momma said he was never the same as he deteriorated from there on. When I came to know him, Alzheimer's disease had inflicted its wrath. His incoherency always left me a little uneasy to be alone with him. I remember Momma saying how hurt she was when he stopped recognizing her. Once she remembered a day when, amazingly, he came out of his "stupor," looked at her and said, "Marg, good to see you. How are you doing?" His coherent smile melted her heart. Regretfully, it only lasted a moment as he lapsed quickly back into the mental prison of the disease.

Most of my memories of him center on the times he and I would sit together on their front porch swing and talk. I would often ask him where he got the gold ring on his finger, knowing well it was his wedding band. With heartfelt conviction he would respond with the most amazing "tall tales," which were so far from the truth it was hard not to chuckle. I wondered how Big Momma ever was able to manage taking care of him. Little did I know how founded in reality that thought was.

I was in high school and I had just started driving. It was early one evening when I had returned home and noticed a note on the kitchen counter near the phone. *Call Big Momma's house as soon as you get in*, it read. I wondered what Mom was doing there as I dialed the number. Mom answered and said Big Daddy had wandered away from the house and couldn't be found. She wanted me to come down and help look. She had a worried tone to her voice and I tried to calm her by assuring her that he would be found. It wasn't the first time he had done this. Several times he had bolted from the house thinking he needed to return to their home on Grace Street in Churchill. Most of the time, Big Momma would catch him before he was off the front porch. This time, however, he was too fast for her.

It took me about forty minutes to drive there from the west end of town. When I arrived I was amazed at the small crowd of people which had gathered in the yard of their small white bungalow, hovering near the porch which spanned the whole front of the house. As I got out of my car, my eyes focused on the porch swing which they had brought from their Churchill house. I had spent many an hour on that swing. I stood still for a minute and drifted momentarily into remembering one of his "tall tales." "Did I ever tell you the time I fell asleep on this swing? While I was snoring, a mouse came up and built a nest in my mouth?" As he explained, he opened his mouth as wide as he could as if to show me how possible it was. In a crowd he was reserved; however, around me his theatrics were as entertaining as his words. He always told me that story as if he had one hand on the Bible and the other raised in an oath. My flashback was suddenly broken by the sound of someone saying "Let's go." I shook my head quickly to refocus and started making my way toward the front door.

I passed by some Boy Scouts milling about under one of the oak trees in the front yard. I found out they had been contacted by a neighbor who had enlisted them to comb some local streets. There were also two policemen with German shepherds waiting to take an assigned area. While talking to them, Mom came out of the house and spotted me. She hurried over and gave me a hug. I had been debating on whether to come at all; however, the look on her face made me realize that I had made the right choice. She told me I had been assigned to be on a three man team which included my cousin Wayne Howard and a neighbor named Sonny. She said other police officers were combing the route to the Churchill area. It was a cold dreary night with on and off rain. Momma said Big Daddy did not have a coat on and would need to be found quickly. So without hesitation, our team, armed with flashlights and ponchos, headed out with a map of the streets we were to cover. Wayne and I were great friends. We often played together at family get-togethers and regularly had sleepovers. This would be a good chance to get reconnected. Besides, talking would keep my mind off my fear of Big Daddy surprising us, stumbling out between two dark houses, or worse coming up from behind and touching us unexpectedly.

Our first "sweep" took us a couple of hours. We looked between houses, in back yards, in and around shrubbery, and out into some nearby farm fields which bordered the housing development. We thought about combing the fields more carefully; however, our first steps were met with calve-high mud. Without boots, it would have been a real struggle. So we looked for footprints or tracks leading out into the field and scanned the area as best we could with our flashlights. We rationalized that no one, not even Big Daddy, would have attempted to cross them.

When we came back to the house to dry off and get a hot drink, we were disappointed that no one had found him. The cold rain had picked up and the concern reflected on everyone's face. Within an hour we were off again to scout out another area. As each hour ticked off, the grim possibilities began edging their way into our conversation. Every two hours we would check in and dry off. By 6:00 a.m. the next morning, with no one reporting any sighting, a depressing pall permeated the house. I was tired. I wanted to get a quick bite of breakfast before heading out again. Wayne and Sonny said they would make a quick sweep and come back to get me.

I was in the kitchen eating, when my uncle Ross came into the house and whispered that Sonny and Wayne had found him dead in a nearby field, not five minutes from the house. The shock of the news confirmed what everyone in the house had been thinking and snuffed out any last flicker of hope. Some went out to the front porch and cried quietly as they thought Big Momma was sleeping in her bedroom. She wasn't. She had heard the quick breaths, the rustling of feet and almost instantly opened her door. She read the dejection on everyone's face and said, "You've found him and he's dead, isn't he?" I don't remember who took the lead in responding but I do remember how Momma and many of her sisters rallied around her as she went back into the bedroom to cry.

I saw Uncle Ross heading for the door. He said he was going back to wait for the coroner. I jumped up and asked to go with him. "Are you sure you want to do this," he asked? "Yes," I said with a firm voice. "I have to see what we missed." He stared at me for a few seconds and with some reluctance said,

"Okay, we'll take my car." As the crow flies, it was a very short distance to the field where he had entered. However, to meet the coroner at the farm house and then get to where Big Daddy lay required driving around to the gate. From there it was a quarter mile drive on a rough dirt road to the furrowed field which was at the back of the property.

When we got out of the car I could see Wayne, Sonny, and a policeman standing out in the field. I started out. With my first step my left leg dropped into the oozing mud up to my calf. When I tried to pull it out my shoe came off! I resigned myself; this is going to take some effort. I pulled my shoe out, put it back on, and plodded on slowly. I curled up my toes which made my loafers fit tighter to my feet. It took about five minutes of some "post holing" to get there. When I finally made it, several times fixing my shoes, I looked down at Big Daddy, lying face up in the mud. He had a slight grimace on his face. I learned he had walked over 120 steps into this muddy field (an amazing show of strength for an elderly man), fallen face down, and then rolled over on his back. The mud was so heavy and sticky he was trapped. He most likely had frozen to death within a few hours. The heat of his body had smoothed the furrowed soil around him. It looked as if someone had taken a small trowel and smoothed a two inch outline around every inch of his body.

I looked at Wayne and said, "We looked out here last night."

"Yes," he responded. "We walked by it several times. But as dirty as he is, we would not have seen him among the furrows. It was only when the sun hit a tip of his blue shirt that Sonny caught it out of the corner of his eye. He had to point to it even after he saw it. It took me a few seconds to see it!"

"All that looking and here he is five minutes from the house. How sad," I murmured.

Shaking his head, Wayne said, "I had a strange feeling he was out in this field." There was great disappointment in his eyes.

Before we could continue, the coroner arrived. As he conducted his examination, all of us were quiet, numbly watching him complete his standard set of protocol. I looked up and saw tears coming down Wayne's face. Up until then I had fiercely kept my emotions in check. But with Wayne's surrender, I had no resistance left. I started sobbing. The kind of crying where you take three or four short sniffles in and then one long one out as you grit your teeth. Uncle Ross reached over and put his arm around me.

"Let's go back to the car," he said in a soft voice. I shook my head wanting to show I could reign in my emotions.

I took a deep breath and said, "I'll be okay." But as soon as I had said it I knew I wasn't going to stop. So within a minute, I started back to the car. He followed soon thereafter. All the way back I kept thinking…what a miserable way to die! I wondered what might have been going on while he laid there. Did he yell out or was he so confused he simply struggled in the mud until he was exhausted and couldn't move any longer? I wondered if he even thought, "this is it. I am going to die." What would that be like? I thought. The whole enormity of it all was weighing on me and I was struggling to come to grips with it.

"Ricky, can I talk with you a minute?" Uncle Ross asked as he came to where I sat looking out the passenger side window of his car.

"Yes sir."

"Let's not let on what we saw in the field this morning. We are just going to tell Big Momma he apparently died of a heart attack."

"You understand don't you?" He put his hand on my shoulder.

"Yes sir, I do."

"Good. We'll just keep it amongst us guys." He then rounded the car and sat down in the driver's seat.

"Are you okay to head back to the house?" He turned over the ignition on his car.

"Yes sir, I'm done crying." I looked up and gave him a determined smile to reassure him of my words.

"I knew I could count on you. You are your father's son."

It was another page turning day. It was also one of those "Tattoos" that left an Edgar Allen Poe type of entry into my consciousness and brutally expanded my definition of horror. It was a night and a day that gave birth to a whole new set of emotions that continuously clashed inside my stomach.

It was, more than anything else, one of those moments when innocence walked out the door and stark reality boldly stepped in and took its chair.

"Psssst! Hey, are you in there?"

I was in my room, the front bedroom of our house. It was eight o'clock at night. Who in the world, I thought, would be whispering to me through the window? Mom and Dad were watching television in the den. I was listening to WLEE radio station play the top ten records on the chart. The Beatles had held the top five spots last week and I couldn't wait to hear if they would hold on to them.

"Hey Ricky, are you in there?"

This time I knew the voice. It was Richard, a good friend of mine from high school. I leaned over to the window and said, "Richard, what the heck are you doing in our front bushes?" I heard some laughter from other voices.

"Who else is with you?" I asked.

"Donald and Blake. We're going to drive up to Washington D.C. to hit a night club. We wanted to know if you wanted to come."

"It's eight o'clock at night. Are you crazy?"

"Aw, come on. Where's your sense of adventure?" He chided. "It's going to be a blast. Think about it. We'll be hitting the big city, dancing with some city ladies and making it a night to remember."

Famous last words, I thought. This has all the markings of trouble and trouble followed Richard like a hungry mosquito. But before I could dismiss it in my mind, the thought of heading to D.C., visiting a nightclub for the first time, and just saying that I had done it, started to sound daring. I loved daring. Daring is one of those "merit badges" you go after to include in your repertoire when sitting at the lunch table in school.

"What time do you think we'll be back?" I whispered.

"We should hit the Richmond city limits around two, maybe three o'clock at the latest."

Two or three in the morning! Wow, I thought. This is going to be an adventure. The daring hormones started to kick in. A Washington D.C. nightclub, I thought. Now that will be some story to tell our buddies at "ole Hermitage High."

"Okay, count me in. I just need to think of a story to tell my parents so they won't worry about where I am. I'll be outside in a few minutes."

Before I could think of anything, Dad came into my bedroom which I thought was a stroke of luck. He said that he and Momma were very tired and would be going to bed early. I told him I was going out with the guys soon and would be back in "around midnight." He didn't question me about where I was going, only to be very quiet when I came in so as not to wake them. That would be no problem, I assured him. The only risk I could see was if Dad somehow decided to get up in the middle of the night to get a drink of water and wandered by my bedroom. Then there would have been some real explaining to do as to why I wasn't home by my midnight curfew. This whole adventure was a calculated risk. I knew it.

I had an uneasy feeling as I climbed into Richard's Ford Fairlane. When things started out this easy, trouble seemed waiting for its chance to prove what the poet Robert Burns wrote so aptly: "The best laid plans of mice and men oft go astray." Yet as we arrived in the outskirts of Washington D.C. and made our way into town, I thought maybe Robert would be proved wrong tonight. I should have waited a few more minutes.

When we found the nightclub and got parked on a nearby street, we made our way to the entrance. There was a large "bouncer" standing in the doorway who stopped us and asked for identification. When I heard him say those words, I knew my luck had changed. While he was checking Richard's identification, I whispered to Donald and Blake, "I'm only seventeen. He's checking to be sure we are all eighteen." Donald got a troubled look on his face. "I thought you were eighteen."

"No," I replied. It's a long story. I started first grade at five and have been suffering these types of consequences ever since. I'm going to be bounced."

When Richard finished and saw us lingering he asked what the problem was. I told him I was only seventeen and wouldn't get past the bouncer. Richard, always the wheeler-dealer, tried to ask the bouncer for a "favor." The bouncer folded his arms and in a dead pan tone responded, "No way. No identification means your buddy stays outside."

I made a quick decision. I looked at the guys and said, "You go in and have a good time. I've always wanted to see the White House. I'll kill a couple of hours and then come back." I looked at the bouncer and asked, "How far a walk is it to the White House?" He pointed and said, "About 40 minutes that way."

Richard was the first to respond. "Thanks, Ricky, for being a trooper. We owe you one."

"No problem. Just come out and look for me on the steps in about two hours."

"You got it," Richard said with a smile and a "thumbs up" gesture.

"Oh, by the way, you should have the car keys, just in case". He tossed them to me as he turned and went into the club. Little did he know that this one afterthought would save my life that night.

Okay, I thought, driving would be easier but walking would kill more time. No time like the present to get on my way. I asked the bouncer for some quick directions and headed off.

I was about twenty minutes into the walk when I noticed, two blocks away, a large group of guys lingering on my side of the street. Oh no, a gang I thought. I decided that I'd cross to the other side of the block at the next light. I did. It seemed prudent, especially at 11:00 p.m.

It was good logic but bad common sense. I looked up as I got to the other side and saw the "group" also changing sides of the street. I hoped this was a coincidence. I made another calculated decision. I still had a block to go before running into them. I would change sides again. Trying to look "nonchalant," I crossed at the next light.

I didn't want to look up but I could not hold back. An ugly feeling sank to my stomach. They crossed over again. Now I knew I was in for a confrontation. I thought about just taking off running but knew that had disastrous potential. I rationalized that I could walk right through them as long as I kept my head down and made no eye contact. Robert Burns must have been howling.

Now I was on the same block. Twenty feet, fifteen feet, ten, and then I noticed I was enveloped by the gang. They had let me into their circle but quickly close it behind me. From early glances, there were about twenty of them. There was one guy standing in front of me with a cut off broom handle in his right hand. He must be the leader I surmised. Everyone was quiet. We stood like two gunfighters waiting to see what the other was going to do. The leader was slapping the broom handle into his left hand slowly and deliberately. "If this stick hits you, you are a shit." He then took the stick and hit me with it on my left shoulder. It hurt. I winced but just stared at him.

"Well, I guess I'm a shit," I responded in my most unthreatening voice.

"What the hell are you doing here at this hour?" he growled.

My mind was speculating the kind of beating that was about to happen. I had been in fist fights before but never twenty on one. This had the look of something brutal. Internally, I was bracing for the worst. My heart was pounding in my chest. I hoped they would not kill me.

"Hey, you. Are you going to answer me? What the hell are you doing here?" He took the broom handle and began poking my breastbone. Every cell in my brain was yelling, don't react….don't react….don't react.

"Obviously, I made the worst decision of my life. I came up with some friends to go to a nightclub but couldn't get in without identification. My friends got in. I didn't. I thought I would stroll down and see the White House." I knew he could see the fear in my eyes.

The leader just stared back at me and didn't respond. He kept rhythmically poking my breast bone with the broom handle. I was expecting any minute to be hit across the face with it or a sucker-punch by one of his lieutenants. The silence was deafening.

"We're going to play a little game," the leader remarked slowly. "You like games don't you?"

I remained quiet.

"We're going to give you a thirty second head start and then we're coming after you." His tone of voice was decidedly sinister. "You need to know that we have never lost." I could see that the rest of the gang began moving into position.

"The game starts when you turn around."

There was no time to think. The leader looked at his watch and yelled "go."

I turned and started running down the block. I made an instant plan. I jumped out into the street and ran down the white lines. If they caught me, I thought, they would have to tackle me in the middle of the road. Maybe a car coming down the street would give them pause. I wasn't a block into my run when I heard a loud voice. I turned around and saw them break towards me like bats out of a cave. Now the game was afoot.

I knew I had to beat them to the car. If I kept a lead of one block, I could get to the car, get in and lock the doors, start it, and run over anybody in my way. I knew that my entire cross country running would now be tested. I ran on the balls of my feet, sprinting. I knew the next twenty five minutes would be life or death. This was no time to hold anything back.

I glanced back at every light. I was keeping distance from them. They were running on the sidewalks. This was no time to fall I thought. Any mistake now would be ugly.

About fifteen minutes into the chase I could see their lead runner start too slow up. I didn't. My focus was on getting to the car. When I got there, I was exhausted. Sweat was rolling off my body and the muscles in my legs were screaming with cramps. I jumped into the driver's seat, locked the doors, started the car, and pulled out. I could see small groups of guys walking a few blocks away but didn't need to confirm if it was them. I headed straight for the nightclub. I decided to just circle the block where the nightclub was, lingering each time at the entrance.

For the next hour I reviewed each moment of the terrible encounter. I felt so stupid. What was I thinking? The leader was right. What in the hell was I doing there at that hour? What if Richard hadn't tossed me the keys? Suppose they had caught me?

I was ruminating through the gruesome options when I saw Richard come out of the club and spotted me double parked in the car. As he came up to the passenger side window, I rolled down the window. "We're ready to head home. I'll go in and grab Donald and Blake. You didn't miss much. The band was okay but the girls were a bit snooty." He turned to head back in but suddenly looked back. "Hey, how was your walk to the White House?"

"I didn't make it. I got mixed up on the directions and decided to turn around," I responded faking a yawn. I was embarrassed by my utter stupidity. Sharing it with him would have served no purpose.

"Oh well, nothing ventured, nothing gained, right?" Maybe next time we should try to go to Ocean View or Virginia Beach. I think beach towns have more action."

Once again, a page turned. I heard it turn. I felt the breeze from its turning. It turned my head around all right. I had walked precipitously close to the edge of disaster, and fortuitously was allowed, as they say, to live to talk about it. I humbly walked away with many lessons that night. Among the most poignant, you want to be very careful when you stroll where tattoos do their best work.

NON NOBIS DOMINE

*"We are therefore about to establish a school
of the Lord's service in which we hope to introduce
nothing harsh or burdensome."*

Rule of Saint Benedict, prologue. 480-543 A.D.

I don't think I gave it any serious thought until I entered sixth grade. Even then it didn't strike me as "something to be concerned about" until the ninth grade. It was simply one of those routines of everyday life. The only time it would cross my mind is when the rest of the neighborhood kids would ask why I wore "that blue and white uniform" to school.

Mom was raised Catholic as were her six sisters and four brothers. They all attended St. Patrick's Church and St. Patrick's School on Churchill. St. Patrick's was located very near St. John's Church where Patrick Henry gave his famous "Give me liberty or give me death" speech. Dad, one of eight children, was also raised a Catholic. His mother, Angiolina, was a devout Catholic until her husband, Amedeo, suddenly died of pneumonia. Traumatized with that disaster, she vented her anger on God, taking her children out of the church. She didn't want to have anything to do with a God who could leave her in that position. However, when Dad married Mom at St. Patrick's, he placated her by returning to the church. It was ever apparent to me that he had no zeal for religion and was just going through the motions, following her lead to keep family harmony. We all went to St. Bridget's church every Sunday morning. My brother and I both attended the corresponding parochial school, St. Bridget's Elementary.

The Catholicism that I grew up with was steeped in rules, regulations, observances and religious training. Catechism commanded the daily regimen of the first few grades and was soon followed by the Missal which specified the parts of the mass. In "my day" it was still being conducted in Latin. Beginning in First Grade and continuing each year, the standard curriculum of reading, writing and arithmetic was accompanied by studies in the Holy Ordinances such as: Communion, Confession, Confirmation, Holy Days of Obligation, the Priesthood (Holy Orders), Marriage, and Last Rights (Extreme Unction).

First grade became the embarkation point for sailing into this sea of Roman Catholic theology; my first communion its first voyage. Each ordinance has its own ecclesiastical ceremony and First Communion was no exception. The boys and girls of my class of communicants, dressed all in white, marched in procession to the altar which spanned the front of the chancel. There we knelt down and readied ourselves for the priest to place a thin wafer in our mouth. My friends and I were not focused on the "transubstantiation" (the theological labeling for what the Church proclaimed the wafer represented) before us but concentrated more on doing everything according to what we had been taught. The nuns, ever the taskmasters, would not accept any trifling on such solemn occasions. Strict obedience was an absolute. I knew from experience that as angelic as they looked in their black and white habits, it only masked the swiftness by which they could hand out corporal punishment. They made a "believer" out of me very early on. "Religious right" meant something totally different than from what it means today.

After the ceremony, Mom doted over me and demanded I stand still for what seemed an endless amount of posed pictures. She loved my ensemble: white shoes, white pants, white shirt, white tie, and white suit jacket. It may have been the last time I would have ever appeared to be "saintly." It was no secret that I personified the adage, "appearances can be deceiving." My infamous second grade school picture, the one with the scowl on my face, the one where I looked like I had been caught with my hands in the "cookie jar," was validation of this point. My Aunt Leona used to say I had a "mischievous bent." Dad, forever frank and to the point, would chime in with his sobriquet, "definitely Dennis, the Menace." Mom put a more compassionate spin on her nickname and called me her little "Dickens."

What a perfect segue into the ordinance of confession!

To think of confession, you had to think "Hail Mary," "Glory be to the Father," "Our Father," (Catholicism's way of identifying the Lord's Prayer) and "the Act of Contrition." These were the prayers which were the "utilities." The protocol began when you entered the small closet sized room which had a place for kneeling. As you knelt, you faced what appeared to be an opaque window and waited quietly for the priest. The priest, who sat in an adjacent room, would slide away the opaque cover and listen through the remaining translucent window. The whole process began with your opening line, "Bless me, Father, for I have sinned. It has been (a month or whatever time) since my last confession. I have the following sins I want to confess."

The priest listened to your list and sometimes asked questions or gave you a quick thought. He concluded the dialogue by first stipulating your penance (which varied), "Say the Act of Contrition, ten Our Fathers, ten Hail Mary's, and one Glory be to the Father," followed by "Go in peace."

It was rarely a cathartic experience for me. I was often too embarrassed or too afraid to really divulge my innermost sins. There was rarely a feeling of comfort or mercy for me. Most priests often had a hurried tone to their voice, as if they knew how long the lines were outside. My real confession came afterwards as I knelt in the church completing my penance. It was there that I unloaded what was truly on my heart. I didn't realize the magnitude of it then but the difference in talking directly to God versus through an intermediary began laying its seeds in my subconscious.

The next voyage set sail for the holy rite of "Confirmation." This ordinance, the next step in your growth in the faith, required you to confirm your commitment to God and choose a patron saint, who could serve as a model for your life. The ceremony was even more elaborate than First Communion as it was conducted by the Bishop of the Diocese versus the Rector of the parish church. For the boys the uniform of the day consisted of blue pants, white shirt, blue cardigan sweaters, and red ties. Each boy was partnered with a girl from the class. I was partnered with a girl named Rosemary who I secretly thought looked beautiful in the white veil which delicately outlined her face. With hands folded in prayer, our class walked two by two slowly up the aisle of the church, through the altar gate, up to the Bishop. There he sat solemnly facing the congregation in his special chair, with his miter on his head, long crooked staff in his hand, and multi-colored ornamental robes. He was surrounded by a number of priests in their regalia and altar boys with their black and white tunics. The smell of incense permeated the air. Organ music and young tenor voices rang out from the choir loft. It was an amazing presentation of ecclesiastical solemnity and formality. The whole front of the church… from the trays of candles near the altar rail flickering in their translucent red and green glass holders, to the statues of St. Bridget and Paul the Apostle, which stood near the gate to the altar, to the whole marble altar that was filled with gold and silver chalices, gold plates, large Bible, larger candles on four foot pedestals, the polished carved wooden facade that served as a backdrop for the altar, the wooden cross with crucified Jesus which was centered on this façade eight feet above the altar, the Renaissance type paintings of the saints which adorned the upper walls, the ornate tapestries, to the small chapels that flanked the main altar area …projected authority, order, formality, tradition, power, and wealth. It took on the perspective of an enormous El Greco painting. The feeling of walking into that picture will stay with me for the rest of my life.

"This is it," I whispered to myself as I knelt in front of the Bishop. Rosemary had gone first. I followed. As he made the sign of the cross with his thumb on my forehead, he bent over and asked, "What saint have you chosen?"

"St. Francis." I answered.

"Of Assisi or Xavier?" I could feel his hot breath on my ear and smell the incense that seemed to permeate his robes.

"St. Francis of Assisi."

"An excellent choice." He flashed a broad smile as he laid his hand on my head. He then recited a prayer, raised his right hand and made the sign of the cross over me. As prescribed, I kissed his ring, got up, refolded my hands, reconnected with Rosemary, and we returned to our assigned pews.

I had chosen St. Francis of Assisi after considering many other saints. I had thought seriously of the Apostle Peter but, not having read the Bible, I did not have as strong an identification with him. Today, the choice would have been easy. Peter would have won, hands down. But for that moment in my life, Francis took the day. His commitment to serve the Lord foregoing all wealth, spreading the Gospel, was inspirational. His amazing sense of purpose left me in awe. The fact that St. Francis was one of the few saints, according to Catholic tradition, to receive the "stigmata" (receiving the actual wounds of Christ) near his death as a reward for his life's work, only confirmed that I wanted to know more about this man and the level of dedication that burned in his soul.

Exploring the life of St. Francis was probably the zenith of my Catholic experience. However, it also left its penetrating incongruency. How could I reconcile the life and model of St. Francis, that of complete poverty, with a church which portrayed itself quite differently at my confirmation? When that thought first went through my mind, I shuttered. What was I thinking? Had I turned into a heretic? It was the kind of thought that I knew would get me into trouble. I tried to bury it. It reminded me of a story about a friend of my father who we called "Uncle" Wade. He had been captured at Anzio in Italy during the Second World War. When he first got into the staging area for captives, he noticed that inside his jacket he had a grenade. Realizing that if it was discovered, he would be instantly shot; he carefully dug a hole, and while no one was looking, buried it. I tried to do the same thing with my "grenade." Yet the moment it "climbed onto my radar screen," I knew it wasn't going to leave.

Early on, church doctrine appeared like fenced in playgrounds, built for security. There was never a need to question anything. The nuns were in complete control and it seemed normal to trust them with everything. There was no need to venture out or even look over the fence. In first grade this "playground" seemed as big as a football field and epitomized all the space I thought I would have ever needed.

Yet by seventh and eighth grades, when questions began arising from a weariness of accepting absolutes and obedience strictly at face value, it more resembled a postage stamp. The fence, once a symbol of protection, became a symbol of confinement. I began to feel confused, manacled, and frustrated.

It got worse, much worse.

Mom was adamant that I attend Catholic High School. She would not entertain any discussion about my attending a public high school. I tried to broach the delicate subject once but her "no, absolutely not" was as final as a judge pounding her gavel down against the bench. I knew Dad, from the look on his face, was not yet ready to fight this battle for me. Thus, with all avenues of appeal excruciatingly explored, Benedictine High School became the school of choice, her choice for me. It was a cadet school, where regimentation and draconian discipline became the footings for everyday life. Priests replaced nuns in the classrooms and drove the culture with an iron fist. It was not an uncommon experience to see a priest throw an eraser, piece of chalk or book at a student…or punch a student or grab someone by their hair for any infraction to the rules. Consequences were immediate and harsh. For someone who wanted less structure, more opportunity to "look over the fence" to explore the parameters of the faith, to question the absolutes and search out the justification for its requisites, cadet school felt like a prison sentence. There would be no interrogatories. Basically if you had time for questions, you had too much time on your hands. Asking became a request for extra duty.

Outside the classroom, upper classmen were given the responsibility to "manage" the student body. As a freshman, it was very easy to figure out "where the buck was going to stop." Seniors were given most of the key officer positions. Juniors, next in line, were assigned Company command responsibilities, and sophomores were the platoon sergeants and squad leaders. Freshmen held the rank of private and served as the target of a great deal of hazing.

Each day began with the same morning military formation. It was scripted much like a play. Eight companies assembled outside the school building. A company consisted of two or three platoons of approximately 30 cadets. The platoons were broken down into three squads of ten cadets.

My company commander would bark out, "Company, attention. Open ranks, march. Close intervals, dress right dress. Ready, front." There I stood at attention in A Company dressed in my West Point grey with black stripe uniform, small black billed military cap, spit shined shoes, and polished brass waiting to be inspected by the First Sergeant, Platoon Lieutenant, and Company Captain. Failure to pass inspection resulted in demerits. Demerits were an interesting form of discipline, which I will discuss in the coming paragraphs. If there was time, each company captain would call out a command to close ranks and then proceed to march in parade formation around the field. Close order drills (right flank, left flank, to the rear, column left, etc.) were also practiced.

At eight o'clock the second act would begin. All companies had returned to their position on the parade ground.

The Battalion Commander and his staff would march out to the formation and face the companies. The Battalion Commander would draw his sword and then yell, "Battalion." The Company Commanders, drawing their swords, would instantly respond at the top of their voices, "Company." Continuing the sequence, the Platoon leaders would respond, "Platoons." The Battalion Commander would then yell, "Aten....hut!" (The word "attention" in phonetic military lingo) All the cadets in the eight companies would snap to attention from parade rest. The sound of shoes slapping together filled the morning air and was followed by complete silence in these long grey lines. From the Battalion commander ranks, a bugler would step out. The Battalion commander would yell to all, "Present Arms!" This called all cadets to assume the "salute" position. Standing at attention, your right upper arm would be parallel to the ground and your lower forearm was cocked on a forty five degree angle with right hand barely touching the right edge of the bill of your cap.

The bugler would then commence playing a special rendition of reveille as two other cadets raised the American flag up a towering flagpole which stood near the center of the tarmac. When the flag reached its pinnacle, the Battalion Commander would yell, "Order arms," which meant a release of your salute and a return to the position of attention.

"Report" was his next command. In sequence, each company officer would raise his sword in salute and reply, "A Company all present and accounted for; B Company all present and accounted for" and so on until each company had responded. The echo of their voices reverberated across the formation.

After ordering the battalion to stand at parade rest, the Battalion Commander would order another officer to step out of the battalion staff formation, come to attention in front of the battalion, face the companies, and read the special orders of the day. Finally, the Battalion Commander would release his command to the company commanders.

"Company dismissed," was the last command of the morning formation. Everyday, those words were music to my ears even though I knew the same type of formation would close the day. With just a few minutes to get to class, I ran to my locker, left my cap, and grabbed my books. Latin I, a review of Caesar's Gallic Wars, was my first period start to the day. How appropriate I thought! The book begins with "all Gaul is divided into three parts." I used to fantasize humorously that Julius Caesar was wrong. There had to be more than three parts. After all, every upperclassman had obviously apportioned a part of it! You could see the evidence of the arrogant "gall" in their faces.

It was all the regimentation, discipline, and hazing I didn't want to have, especially after the eight years I had spent at St. Bridget's Elementary. I was struggling and I knew it. The key word for my freshman year became endurance. The key questions surrounding endurance became…How much abuse could I stand? What kind of wall could I construct around my psyche that would not allow any upperclassman to get the best of me? How quickly could I learn to tune out an upperclassman screaming obscenities two inches from my face? Callousness was essential to endurance. Mental toughness was vital to survival. Any show of emotion or feeling was a sign of weakness and identified you as a target. "Targets" were hunted down for the sheer fun of it.

I caught on quickly. After all, I grew up with an older brother who used me as a testing ground for every trick, every practical joke, and every form of subtle torture that ever came down the pike. Thanks to him, I was "street smart" by the third grade and had developed a keen eye for incoming abuse. It is the good news and bad news of having an older brother.

The problem or knot that kept forming in my stomach was that the classroom environment moderated by the priests never offered a respite from the gauntlets laid out by the upperclassmen. I felt like I was in a rose bush. Everywhere I turned I was getting stuck by sadistic absurdity.

As far as it's being a contest of wills, I knew I could endure. I felt like I could push myself to any length to "not give in." The problem wasn't how to endure or if I could…it was why should I? Perhaps for the first time in my school life, I was questioning the Catholic rationale. What purpose were they trying to achieve? Whom were they trying to serve? The "El Greco" paintings I had once held in awe were starting to get a "Velasquez" type of disfigurement to them. Discontentment began stirring the resentment in my soul.

The ultimate reality of this feeling came in late spring of my freshman year. I had gotten six demerits from an upperclassman officer for, in his mind, "trifling." I wasn't trifling but quickly understood it was his form of hazing. Demerits had to be worked off. This required showing up for a detention class on Saturday morning and copying in cursive handwriting pages from a military manual. One demerit required copying three pages of the manual. Each page, full of small print, took about thirty minutes to copy. I worked off three of the demerits in one grueling session. Lamenting that I had three more, I asked if there was any other way to work off demerits. I was told there was another way: "Drumsticks." Drumsticks meant going into a room, pulling down your pants and, while bending over, allowing a priest to deliver three stinging blows against your buttocks for each demerit. Nine, I thought. What was worse? Should I choose four and a half more hours on a Saturday morning of copying the most ridiculous inane sentences that I had ever read or enduring perhaps three or four minutes of excruciating pain? I chose the pain, counting on my strong threshold of tolerance to endure.

I remember its being a late Friday afternoon. The room, barely lit by the sun, was shaded to suit the occasion. The priest stood there gently slapping a wooden drumstick in his hand. The upperclassman who had given me the demerits was also standing in the room with a degenerate smirk on his face.

The priest coldly said, "Drop your pants, bend over, and grab the desk." Determined not to cry or utter a sound, I complied. The moment of truth had arrived. The first three went relatively quickly as I closed my eyes, clenched my jaw shut, and stubbornly showed no emotion, only flinching. I could feel this infuriated the priest. He paused after number three, deliberately slowed his pace and increased his force on number four. Numbers five, six, and seven were harder still. I almost let out a scream but held on even tighter to the desk. "Eight…and nine, and then suddenly…ten!" the priest shouted as if he was competing with my will to resist. It was done. I took a deep breath. My butt was numb with pain. "Get dressed," the upperclassman barked. Showing no emotion, I tenderly pulled up my pants and stood facing them. He pointed the drumstick at my face and said, "I gave you one extra for good measure. I better not find you back in here. Next time will be worse." I caught myself from saying what was on my mind. I simply gave him the sterile reply, "You will never see me in here again, Father." It was one of the defining moments of my life. Father McDonnegal may have thought he drummed into me some discipline but he was wrong. What he did was beat into me a fierce recognition of what I now knew I hated about the church. I vomited up what I could not hold down any longer. Catholicism was not about serving God; it was about serving "the church." It wasn't about nurture and mercy; it was about subjugation. Worst of all, the attitude of the ends justify the means became pervasive and a license for some sickening misanthropic behavior. His "one for good measure" had slammed the door on reconciliation and permanently fueled the fire of my infuriation. I drew a mental "line in the sand." I left school that day resolved that I would do anything, absolutely anything, to leave Catholic school and never come back.

I began a summer persuasion campaign to influence my parents which would have made even the Roman orator Cicero proud. On this subject, there was not a doubt that my father was the more pliable of the two. My mother was raised a devout Catholic. She was committed beyond reason to seeing her children raised in the church. Her mother had handed her this tradition. It was ingrained, virtually impervious to change. My father, although raised in the church, had encountered a much different experience, explained earlier. I pleaded with him to let me go to school with my neighborhood friends. My Dad was forever giving me the advice to "be one of the guys. Get along with everyone." I seized upon his words and kept reiterating that I wanted the chance to be just one of the guys in the neighborhood and not be the only one attending Catholic School. As General Grant did to Lee, I brought the "war" to him every single day, hoping beyond hope that attrition was the right end game.

I never knew what the final convincing argument was. All I can remember is one August afternoon he fell silent during one of our tête-à-têtes. He stared at me for a few minutes and after a long sigh said, "Okay. You can go to Hermitage High School. I will work it out with your mother. Leave that part to me."

My Dad and I didn't have a "hugging type of relationship". He didn't like the "lovey-dovey" stuff. But that day, I threw my arms around him and repeatedly thanked him. I knew Mom would offer up strong resistance. But I also knew Dad's look and decision were irreversible.

If hope springs eternal, then release must be a geyser! I was delirious. My soul screamed, "Go tell the people of Mudville that the mighty Casey was coming back to the plate!" If I had known the old Negro spiritual, as Dr. Martin Luther King suggested, I would have sung it at the top of my lungs... "Free at last, free at last, thank God almighty, I am free at last."

AND LEAD US NOT INTO TEMPTATION...

"And sometimes we are devils to ourselves
When we tempt the frailty of our powers,
Presuming on their unchanged potency."

Troilus and Cressida IV, iv, 95. William Shakespeare.1601-1602

Just the mention of the word barbecue makes my mouth water. Say it again and what flashes into my mind are pictures of a restaurant that makes the best shredded pork barbecue sandwich in the world. Bill's Barbecue got its start in Richmond. Its first establishment was near Boulevard and Broad Street, just around the corner and not far from Julian's Pizza. I am letting you in on one of my memorization techniques. My way to remember places around town was connected to where there were some of the best places to eat! When you are a teenager, and can consume twice your weight in food daily, this is important stuff. Okay, that may be a slight exaggeration but you get the point.

Bill's first expansion was near the intersection of Libby Avenue and Broad Street; 5500 Broad, to be exact. When we lived on Horsepen Road and later when we lived on Bethlehem Road, we were less than ten minutes away. I used to conjecture that a strong southerly wind could blow the "heavenly" smell over to our Bethlehem Road house.

Bill's Barbecue had a typical diner look about it. It was a one room building with some bar stools and tables. If you wanted service in your car, you backed into your parking space and turned on your headlights. The waitress would come to your car, take your order, and then return with an aluminum tray arrayed with your food. The tray was engineered to rest just outside the driver's side window. The "cool" part about eating outside was you could eat, talk with your date, and watch to see who else was coming through the lot. Most of the cars coming through were "cruisers." They weren't coming to eat anything; they just wanted to check out to see who was there and show off their cars. It was not unusual to sit there for a couple of hours and watch the "parade." It was the thing to do on Friday night after the football game. First you surfed through McDonalds, then Shoney's Big Boy, but you stopped at Bill's. Burgers were good but nothing could compare to those shredded pork barbecues, with cole slaw and a touch of Tabasco sauce. I would normally order three, a large order of fries, a plain water limeade, and a piece of their special strawberry pie. In my high school years the cost of a barbecue was thirty five cents! With or without a date it wasn't expensive and you couldn't quantify the value of the "parade" passing by.

As I remember, it was a weekday morning in the summer. Mom had headed off to work and Dad was about to leave. He made a point of interrupting my breakfast to say, "I don't want you driving your car without getting an inspection sticker. It's your own fault for procrastinating on having your turn signals fixed. I told you two weeks ago it wouldn't pass." My car had failed and the inspection station had scraped off the old sticker. Dad continued his admonishment. "You will get your allowance on Friday and then can take it up to Childress Auto Body on Saturday morning. They can fix it and inspect it all at one time."

He paused. I knew it was for effect. "Listen to me now. I don't want you driving that car and get a ticket. You hear me?"

"Yes sir", I responded quickly, wanting to get back to eating. However, I could see he wasn't finished.

"Now listen to me. No driving means no quick trips...and that includes Bill's Barbecue! You understand, right?" His tone was emphatic.

"I understand."

"Okay, see you tonight. Don't forget to mow the grass and sweep the carport." With that he was out the door and I was back to my Cheerios.

I hadn't planned to go anywhere. I was going to get my chores done and then maybe play some basketball up the street with one of the neighbors. All would have gone well except Dad had unknowingly planted the seed of temptation in me right before he left with his... "And that includes Bill's Barbecue," statement.

From the minute he said it, pictures of those pork barbecues began to periodically interrupt my thoughts. I went out, swept the carport, and began to mow the lawn to see if that would get my mind off of it. Distraction sometimes is a great eraser. It was a valiant attempt but it didn't work. I knew I was in trouble when the grass clippings started to remind me of the chopped cole slaw on top of the shredded pork! Did I mention how it melts in your mouth and is like no other flavor you have ever had? I went inside and washed up.

Then the rationalization process began. You know the one where you try to convince yourself what the real issue is and try to minimize what was really said. What was Daddy's biggest concern? He didn't want me to get a ticket. Well, I could easily take the back roads and make sure I was only on Broad Street for less than a few seconds. Besides, I could get there and be home in less than ten minutes. What are the odds I would even run into a policeman? Daddy's concern was a bit out of proportion to the risk...I thought. After all, if he knew all there was for lunch was peanut butter and jelly, he would have relented and let me go. Sure he would. He probably would have asked me to pick up a couple for him. And he loved those plain water limeades as much as I did. I would have surprised him with a piece of that mouth watering strawberry pie with the thick whipped cream and that "to die for" sugary crust.

Who was I kidding? Was I out of my mind? Daddy would be mad. He made it perfectly clear that he didn't want me driving without an inspection sticker. If he were here, he would have used that same pedantic tone. But you know...parents overreact to situations. They don't understand or really consider the risk. All this would be would be a quick harmless ten minute ride and boom...it would be over. You know it was not like I was thinking of robbing a bank. On the whole scope of things, this really was just a difference of opinion.

You know...I bet I could go up there and get back and prove that there was no cause for alarm. I wouldn't have to tell him until much later, even a few weeks or months. I could wait for just the right time to bring it up.

Maybe I could do such a good job on the yard and even do some extra things that would convince him that I really had my "act together." Maybe if I showed him I was really responsible with my chores, he would say... "You know Ricky; I think you should make your own decisions about things. You have proved to me you are thinking clearly and ready to call all your own shots."

The rationalization came to its climax.

Even if I did go, he would balance his anger with the helpful person I was around the house. I was sure he would understand this small indiscretion. It would be like getting my hand caught in the cookie jar. It would be something we would laugh at in later years.

Now the barbecue pictures and smells were picking up momentum in my mind. Okay, I thought, "Bill's here I come."

I headed east on Bethlehem road, turned right on Libby Avenue and kept my eyes peeled for any car which might have had an official look to it. Within three minutes I was approaching Broad Street. I gave a quick look both ways, made my right turn, accelerated rapidly and turned in Bill's. Whew, four minutes...not bad I thought. I parked my '57 Volkswagen face in so that by chance if a police car came through the lot he would not see my front windshield. As I entered Bill's, I thought, why should I be in a hurry? Dad wasn't going to be home until dinner. I should just eat my meal inside, in case I wanted seconds on anything. Besides, there was no need to leave any evidence around the house. All I would need is to have Daddy take out the garbage and fortuitously see barbecue wrappers. No, the better idea was to eat at Bill's. So I did. I savored every bite. I was in heaven. With the last slurp of my limeade, I got back into my car. I circled Bill's parking lot and was ready to sneak across Broad Street and head for home.

All I had to do was a right turn on Broad Street, go a half a block and make my left on Libby Avenue and I was virtually home free. Broad Street is four lanes and I was in the left lane heading east. Everything seemed like it was going to plan...until the light at Libby Avenue turned red. It was a little frustrating because it would keep me out on Broad longer than I wanted. I stopped. As I eagerly waited for it to change, disaster struck; a police car appeared unexpectedly. I didn't see it coming. It was hidden from my view by a truck which was heading westbound. I told myself, don't panic. The two policemen are busy talking. They won't look over into the eastbound lane. I kept staring at the light begging it to change. I decided not to turn at Libby Avenue as that would have taken me right in front of them. I would head east for one block and make my turn there. I started whispering, "Hurry up light, hurry up light." I saw the light which controlled the Libby traffic change to yellow. Finally, I thought the Broad Street signal would soon turn green. "Come on, come on," I mumbled as I glanced over at the police car. Just a split second before the light turned green, the passenger side policeman finished his conversation with the driver and casually looked over at my car. It was instantaneous. I saw him raise his hand and point at my car. I could read his lips as he said, "Look, no inspection sticker on that Volkswagen!" The light turned green. My heart sank. O no, I was going to get a ticket. Daddy would have a field day with me. He was right all along. I wished there was some way for all of this not to happen. Wasn't there some way? Options raced through my mind. Rationalization under pressure exponentially increases the amount of stupidity of the thinking process. It is a theorem I have unfortunately proved numerous times in my life. What I am about to describe is one of my early proofs.

Because Broad Street had a median in this part, I knew that the policemen had to go westbound for a bit before they could do a U-turn to come back and pull me over. I made my turn at Libby but then turned right into a housing development which was just off Broad. Maybe, just maybe, they wouldn't see me make the left turn on Libby or if they did, the right turn one block later. My heart started pounding. When you mess up, you understand the consequences. However, sometimes you hope you can get a reprieve.

I drove quickly into the development and started making left and right turns every block or so to "lose myself" as an extra precaution. I kept looking into my rear view mirror to see if my tactic worked. I thought about pulling over and parking between two trucks in an effort to hide but decided the further I could get from Broad Street the better.

No police car was in sight; so far so good. I then made a dash for Bethlehem Road. I knew from where I would turn on to it, it was about a one mile shot to our house. I slowly approached Bethlehem and stared both ways to make sure the police car wasn't on it. I waited a few more minutes and then decided to make a run for it. I pulled out and "put the pedal to the metal." For me it was like the top of the stretch run at Churchill Downs. It was the "run for the roses." The only thing funny about it was I was in a '57 Volkswagen. Who was I kidding? I could "wind it out" through all four gears but I would still only be traveling at about fifty miles per hour!

As I went past the development I had crisscrossed through, I repeatedly jerked my head to the left to glance down each of the streets as a final check to see if I was safe. "No police car…no police car," I uttered much like a pilot going through a checklist. Then, on the last street before Libby Avenue, my heart stopped. There it was. The police car was making its way rapidly through the development! I knew it would be only a matter of seconds before they hit Bethlehem Road and would see me. At best I would have a ten second lead.

Panic set in. My stupidity meter correspondingly registered new levels of insanity.

Bethlehem Road is straight in this section. You head downhill for most of it but right before our house there is a hill. If I could get over the hill, I would be out of sight for a few seconds. In those critical few seconds, I could make a right turn into our driveway, drive across our front yard, sneak around the left side of the house, careful to avoid hitting the short white ornamental fence, and drive into the back yard. With any luck the policemen would drive by the house. Then this whole horrible fiasco would be over.

I shifted out of first gear at twenty five, ten miles an hour over the recommended mark on the speedometer. I left second gear at forty; third gear at fifty five. The high pitch sound from my Volkswagen engine was like an old Singer sewing machine trying to run at supersonic speed.

As I crossed the small bridge at the bottom of the hill and headed up, I looked into my rear view mirror and saw the police car swerve onto Bethlehem Road. They had seen me. The front end of the police car rose quickly as it accelerated.

"I have got to get behind our house unseen," I said to myself. I got ready to down shift as I approached our driveway. I came over the hill at about 65 miles an hour, shoved the gear shift into third and popped the clutch getting ready for a "power turn."

Up until this point, I was fairly sure that I had thought of everything; at least everything I could have relative to the circumstances and the stress of the moment. That should have been my first and biggest clue. I was adept at reading the tachometer, the speedometer, the gear I was in, the slope of the road...but I hadn't taken a glance at the "stupidometer." If I had I would have pulled over and stopped the madness.

However, irrational panic was sitting on the throne of my behavior, not logic. Up came the driveway to our house. The moment of truth had arrived.

My Dad worked hard every day of his life. He not only supported our family, he also provided some financial support to his brothers and sisters when they needed it. He committed himself to "rolling up his sleeves" early on and never complained. I don't ever remember on a weekday his coming home for lunch…well, almost never. Of all of his brothers, the one that was the toughest disciplinarian was Uncle Raymond. He was a good guy but not the guy you wanted around when you made a mistake. He knew, in his own special way, how to bring things to order in a hurry. He and his wife Virginia, a delightful person, would pop over to visit us occasionally on weekends, rarely on a weekday.

I guess you would have to ask yourself what were the odds that Daddy would come home for lunch. Compound those odds with Uncle Raymond stopping by to join him…and add on even longer odds that they would be sitting on the front porch eating their sandwiches. I don't ever remember Daddy eating outside. He always ate in the kitchen, dining room, or the den. He wasn't a "picnic" type person. He was the "let's eat" and then get back to work type.

With all of those odds in mind, think also about the odds of a '57 Volkswagen sedan making a power turn in gravel. Volkswagens have no weight up front. The trunk is located in the front of the car. At fifty miles an hour its "power turning" capacity on a normal road is limited. In gravel…it's best to use a quote from Dante's Inferno… "Enter here and abandon hope."

I popped the clutch. The engine screamed even louder under the tremendous compression as it tried to cope with the downshift. It sounded as dramatic as a jet engine being reversed on a runway to slow the plane down. I turned right, hit the gravel of our driveway and began to slide. Surprised by the screeching tires, the thunderous sound of the deceleration, and my car hitting the gravel, my father and Uncle Raymond shouted some expletives, dropped their sandwiches, and started scrambling backwards as fast as they could. Uncle Raymond, who was sitting on the top step almost backed right through the screen on our front door. I slid passed the front porch, desperately trying to gain control by turning back into the slide. I missed hitting the corner of the house by a foot, but did run straight through the ornamental white fence, sending scraps of lumber high into the air. By some miracle, I didn't slide into the deep gully on the side of our house. At the last second my desperate steering wheel correction worked. My Volkswagen caught hold of itself and leapt straight down the side of our house. I turned into the back yard and ended up under the clothes line.

Five seconds later, the police car with its overhead lights on and traveling at a high rate of speed, passed by the house, not noticing the tire tracks across our front yard or the scattered shreds of the white fence on the north side of our house.

I was drained but bracing for the tirade that I knew was coming. "This is going to be ugly," I murmured to myself. "No tap dancing is going to get me out of this one."

I would have to face the anger of my father, egged on by his brother, the king of the disciplinarians.

I locked both of my car doors and just sat there.

Within moments, Daddy and Uncle Raymond were standing at the car window. Daddy tried to open the door and found that I had locked it. "Open the door," he commanded in an angry tone. In the background Uncle Raymond was already giving Daddy the litany of "if he were my son" type of comments in rapid succession.

"Ricky, open this door."

I stared at him. "Daddy, can we talk about what just happened first?"

"Open the door, now." I could tell from his tone that opening the door at that moment was akin to suicide.

"No sir, not while you and Uncle Raymond are this angry." I used the most respectful tone I could muster.

My apparent defiance outraged Uncle Raymond. He got more animated and continued his "if he were my son" comments a few inches from Daddy's ear. Daddy paused for a few seconds. He then looked at Raymond and asked him to let him talk with me alone. Over Uncle Raymond's objections, Daddy insisted with a "please, this is a father and son issue." Uncle Raymond walked back toward the front yard shaking his head as he went.

"Okay, tell me what happened." Daddy was pursing his lips.

This was no time to tell anything but the God's honest truth. I gave him a play by play without leaving out anything. "That's the whole truth, and I am really, really sorry."

"Give me your driver's license." Daddy demanded.

"Yes sir."

Still a little unsure of what might happen if I opened the door, I rolled down the window just enough to slide my driver's license through the crack. Daddy took it and growled, "Don't ask for it back until the grass grows over the tire tracks in the front yard and the fence is repaired. Even then, we still need to have a discussion."

He left with a deliberate pace. I could tell he was still fuming inside. I decided it would be wise to sit in my car for a long while. Finally the "stupidometer" worked its way out of my subconscious and I realized how insane I had been. I think the thing that made me feel the worst was that I had "misbehaved" in front of one of Daddy's brothers. I knew I had put him in a very awkward position. After his father died, he became the father of his family. He worked hard every day to be an example to all of them. I had not helped "the cause." It was one thing to tarnish my own reputation, it was quite another to tarnish my father's. That lesson alone made it a page turning day.

In the following years, Daddy and Uncle Raymond embellished the story considerably as they told it over and over to the laughter and astonishment of many members of the family. They had great fun at my expense. I never objected to their histrionics. I deserved every bit of it and took it in the nature it was given.

Bill's Barbecue still makes the most succulent pork barbecues in the world. The smells coming out of their establishment will always have a "sirenesque" quality to them. (In the book "The Odyssey," Odysseus avoided the Sirens by tying himself to the mast of his ship.)

Perhaps the real lesson of the day, which would have served me well on many other days, had I learned it well, was to learn when and where to tie myself to a tree!

EPITAPH: A LESSON FOR A LIFETIME

*"One word frees us of all the weight and pain of life:
That word is love."*

Sophocles. C 495-406 B.C. Oedipus at Colonus, I.

As a child I considered them my most valuable possession. No, it wasn't my Dell Comic Book collection, my baseball cards, or even my Lionel train set. It was forty nine silver dollars I had collected over a period of ten years from Mom and Dad for birthdays, special occasions and Christmas. About forty of them were "Morgan's" and the rest were "Peace" dollars. Dates on them ranged from the 1870's to the 1920's. Some had mint marks from San Francisco, Denver, Carson City, and New Orleans. Most of them were in good condition. Some of them were in excellent condition. I loved the feel of them. They were heavy and felt substantial in my hand. When they clinked together you could hear these were no ordinary coins. It was fun to spread them over my bed and arrange them by decades.

My brother had numerous coin collections: pennies, nickels, dimes, quarters, and some special dollar bills. He had "blue books," special coin collecting books, with slots for coins from each year. Helping him fill in each year and each mint mark for that year in the little blue books was exciting. I remember exchanging dollar bills for rolls of coins at nearby stores and sifting through them for certain years and mint marks.   It was a red letter day when we came across a coin he didn't have. His exuberance was infectious. I had this "ultimate dream" about finding a "1909 svbd" mint marked penny! I knew it would have been a million to one type of find, as it was extremely rare….but it never stopped me from looking quickly at every coin I received in change. My brother had taught me over and over…just look…you never know.

My brother has eagle eyes and common sense. He also has this gift of being at the right place at the right time. I am sure they are interconnected. His common sense calibrates his eyesight. It is the only way I can explain the hundreds and hundreds of times he has come across rare coins, or uncovered incredible finds at yard sales, estates sales, and thrift stores. His prowess is legendary and could fill another whole book! The one that confounded me when growing up was his ability to find a four leaf clover…on demand. Yes, for twenty five cents (he always bet me a quarter) he would boast he could find a four leaf clover in a few minutes. I took this bet more times than I wish to recall and, to my constant amazement, lost every single time! He would calmly walk around in our back yard and within minutes…come up with one! He told me once "how to do it," even walked me through the process, but I only got frustrated when I couldn't see what he so easily could. I simply stopped trying and accepted his genius. If you are looking for something, he is the guy you want with you.

I didn't have to be told by my brother that the silver dollars were truly worth something. The way he cocked his eyes every once in a while told me I was sitting on something valuable.

When I got my forty-ninth silver dollar I decided it was time to find a place to hide them for safe keeping. I found the ideal spot. One afternoon after school, when no one else was home, I was playing with some marbles in the living room. One slid under the antique Zenith radio-phonograph console. When I pulled the console out from the wall to get it, I noticed that there was an empty space in the speaker box. The second I saw the space, I knew it was the perfect size for the container that held the silver dollars. I ran and got them and eased them in cautiously. I was delighted at how obscure they were in its recesses. I carefully made sure I pushed the cabinet back into the same spot. "Perfect," I whispered. "Absolutely perfect. You would have to get directly behind it before you would notice the container." I was quite proud of my discovery.

One night at the kitchen table Dad said, "I went into your bedroom today and I noticed your silver dollars were gone. You haven't spent them have you?"

"No sir," I quickly responded. "I hid them in the perfect hiding place."

"Where are they?" he said sternly.

"Dad, it's a secret!"

"Well, I hope that hiding place is in the house. I don't want them outside anywhere. That is a lot money." There was a distinct gravity in his voice.

I just kept eating.

"Are they in the house or not?" I recognized his demanding tone. I knew he would not take silence for an answer. He was using his serious voice and that meant he expected a respectful answer, nothing glib.

"Yes sir, they are in the house." I hoped that would put an end to his interrogation.

Something in his facial expression told me he had more to say but he caught himself and resumed eating. I started to feel real uncomfortable but didn't know what to do with the tension that remained in the air. The occasional rattling of silverware hitting our plates became the only sound. I gobbled down my food and then asked to be excused. Dad nodded.

For the next couple of weeks, I decided that the best thing to do was just leave the silver dollars where they were. I still had no idea why they had become the "center of attention." Whatever it was, I thought producing them right away would only open the discussion again and maybe move to where they should be kept. Even worse, I conjectured the discussion would drift toward who should be their guardian.

Within a couple of weeks, the smoke seemed to have cleared. Dad had not brought up anything regarding them. I got the urge to look at them again, and pulled them out of the back of the console before anyone else got home. I shoved them under my bed with the thought of pulling them out sometime after dinner. I made a big deal of pulling them out from under the bed so as to demonstrate that they were always there. I spent the last hour before "lights out" lying on my bed examining the faces of "Lady Liberty" on the Peace dollars. My brother, whose passion for restoring old cars was intense, sat on his bed reading the latest Car Craft magazine hot off the press. Dad came by and stopped at our door.

"It's time to hit the hay guys."

"Yes sir." We both chimed in respectfully.

I decided to test the waters on how he felt about the silver dollars. "Have you ever looked at the crown on Lady Liberty's head up close? It is really cool." I handed him the 1924 silver dollar I had in my hand.

He stared at it a few seconds and said, "It is nice, isn't it?" He handed it back to me but not with the excitement I had hoped. No, he had that same serious face he had at the kitchen table two weeks before. He said "It's time to brush your teeth and hit the hay. Tomorrow is a school day." As soon as he said it he was off to his bedroom.

I looked over and interrupted my brother, "What's wrong with Daddy?"

He looked up over his magazine with a quizzical look on his face and replied, "What?"

"Have you noticed anything funny about him lately?"

"No, not really. Why?"

"Daddy and I got into it two weeks ago over the silver dollars." I whispered for fear Dad may hear me. "He wanted to know where I hid them. I told him I had a secret place."

"I don't get the point. What's the big deal about where you hide them?" He said it so loud I winced. I put my finger to my lips asking for quiet. I got up from my bed and carefully closed our bedroom door. I came back around and sat facing him on my bed.

"I don't know. That's the point! He made this big deal about keeping them in the house. I told him that's where they were," I continued, whispering and looking back occasionally at the door.

My brother leaned over and turned on the radio which lay on the table between our beds. I mimed with my lips…. "Good idea" and held up my thumb to indicate approval. We always tuned in WLEE before cutting out the lights. It would let Dad know, one thin wall away, that we were turning in. Better still, it would give us less of a chance to be heard.

"I think you are making way too much of this. Dad just doesn't want you to lose them. You know it's a lot of money, especially for a twerp like you." He started jabbing me in the side with his finger. "Anyway, where are you hiding them?" He raised his eyebrows and gave me an interrogative smile.

"You can bet that I'm not telling you, Dad or anybody."

"Oh yeah?" he said tauntingly. He jumped on me, got me in a headlock and started rubbing my head with his knuckles. "I bet I can make you tell me."

"Come on Teddy. Let me go." I struggled to get out of his hold but he was much too strong for me. I knew that I had to resort to extreme measures. I yelled, "Ouch, that hurts!"

Mom opened the bedroom door and stuck her head in. "What's the problem?" Good ole Mom, I thought, always saving the day. I took quick advantage of the moment and pulled Teddy's arms off of me and stood up.

"Nothing. We are just having fun wrestling." Rule number one: never "rat" on your brother. Rule number two: "Ratting" on your brother doubles the abuse next time. Rule number three: if he is your hero, put up with a little guff.

"Ricky, pick up those silver dollars. Tomorrow is a school day. It's time to cut off the lights and get to bed," she said with her "I love you but let's get going" voice.

"Yes Ma'am."

"Come here; let me give you a kiss. Teddy, you too". She started to pick up the silver dollars and I stopped her. "Mom, please stop. Let me do that."

"All right, but hurry it up." With that she closed the door.

"You're lucky. One more minute and I would have gotten it out of you," barked my brother.

"You think so?"

"I know so!" His mocking tone struck a nerve. I knew that I had to distract his determination or he would resume his onslaught. I latched on to what I thought was a great idea.

"Well, I've got a deal for you. Tomorrow I'm going to put them back in their hiding place and let's see if you can find them."

With a sinister grin he responded, "You've got a deal. Get ready to lose."

I picked up the rest of the silver dollars, put them in the container and slid them under my bed. I took off my jeans and tennis shoes, slipped on my pajama bottoms and reached up to cut off the light.

It was a surprisingly hot Virginia spring night. Dad had turned on the big house fan he had inserted in the dining room window. The breeze coming in our bedroom window felt good. Teddy and I lay there quietly. WLEE was playing a recording from a southern comic named Brother Dave Gardner. We giggled and laughed at his hilarious routine on David and Goliath.

"Time to shut it down," Dad yelled from his bedroom. Teddy turned off the radio. He whispered as he rolled over on his side, "I can't wait to find those silver dollars." I didn't respond.

All day long at school the next day I couldn't wait to get home and return the silver dollars to the Zenith console. In that speaker box, I surmised, not even my eagle eye brother would discover them. I chuckled. My brother may be the best at a lot of things but this time I liked my chances to come out ahead.

When Alvin our bus driver opened the door, I jumped out of my seat. "What's your hurry?" he asked as I ran up the aisle.

"I've gotta win a bet with my brother."

"Uh oh," Alvin lamented. "I smell trouble coming. Your brother knows his stuff."

"I'll grant you that. But today, I have a plan that cannot fail."

"Famous last words," Alvin decried shaking his head. "Let me know who wins."

I bounded off the bus and ran around the white picket fence, through the backyards of our neighbors and into the backdoor of our house. I took off my backpack and laid it on the kitchen floor. I stopped by the refrigerator to see if there were any of Mom's chocolate chip cookies left and grabbed a glass of milk. Plans were important but not as important as cookies dipped in milk. Besides, my brother wasn't due to be home for at least an hour.

After a few quick bites and slurps, I headed for our bedroom. I knelt down, reached under the bed and couldn't feel the container. I thought that was strange. I was sure I was reaching in the right spot. After a couple of frustrated sweeps with my arm, I bent over, pulled up the bed spread and looked.

My heart stopped. There was no container under my bed. Immediately I started reconstructing what happened last night and this morning. And then it hit me. "Teddy!" I said. "He left for school first but must have sneaked in later and hid them." I started admonishing myself how stupid I had been.

Well, I determined, all was not lost. I would literally scour the whole house room by room before he got home. When I found them, I would then execute my plan and would teach him a lesson about underestimating me.

We had a small house maybe 1000 square feet in total. I looked everywhere: our bedroom, Mom and Dad's bedroom, the living and dining room, kitchen and attic. I covered every inch of the house, but to no avail. I even looked behind the console thinking he may have stumbled onto my idea. Still, there were no silver dollars. I surrendered. When he came through the front door, I would declare him the champ. I would take his kidding and be happy that I had them back.

Bounding through the door that afternoon he saw me pacing back and forth in the living room. "What's going on?"

"You know what's going on. I concede. You win. Now give me back the silver dollars."

"What do you mean?" I don't have them. Honest."

"Come on. I said you were the winner. Quit fooling around and give them to me." I didn't care if he heard my exasperation.

"I don't have them!" he replied raising his voice.

"Honest? You don't have them?" I looked straight into his eyes to detect any glint of trickery.

"I told you that I don't have them. Maybe Dad took them. Did you consider that?"

When he said that, I could tell he was serious. He really didn't have them. But why would Dad take them I thought? Wait a minute, Teddy was right. Dad was acting funny about them. Our conversation at the dinner table flashed back in my mind. "That's it," I yelled. "Dad took them." I couldn't wait for him to get home and end the mystery.

Mom came through the door first. I could tell she had had a long day at the clothing factory. She looked tired. As she was taking off her shoes, I asked her, "Mom, do you know where my silver dollars are?" Her response was curt. "Talk to your father." I was caught off guard by her brusque remark.

"What do you mean? What aren't you telling me?"

"Talk to your father," she insisted. This time she gave me "the stare." It was her sign that I should brace myself for some bad news.

"Yes ma'am." I knew, wherever all of this was going, it wasn't going to be good. I went out the kitchen door dejectedly and decided to throw the ball against the back stoop until dinner. It was my way of letting off some steam and retreating to my own world. With a ball in hand, I could take out my anger on the stoop and get some baseball practice in at the same time.

"Ricky, time for dinner. Come on in and wash up," Mom called from inside the kitchen.

Well, Dad must be home, I thought. I had an awful feeling in my stomach. I wasn't very hungry. I had even come to the point of not wanting to talk about the silver dollars. I had thought about all the bad possibilities and didn't want whatever final news there was. Getting "final news" about something, meant all possibilities were over. I knew it was going to be one of those "you'll understand someday" kinds of discussions. I wasn't ready for it.

"Bless us, O Lord, for these thy gifts for which we are about to receive from thy bounty through Christ our Lord," Mom recited. We all responded in unison, "Amen." She had fixed spaghetti with meat sauce, a staple at our house.

"I know you love spaghetti, Ricky, so dig in. Do you want a slice of bread?" That was my mother, always trying to soften the blow that was coming my way; always trying to make the best of a not so good situation. I knew it would not be long before I would find out what happened to the silver dollars. The whole meal had the tenor of "a last meal" a prisoner gets before his demise.

"May I be excused? I want to go work on my car," Teddy asked. Dad nodded. He bolted from the table. Mom got up and poured Dad a cup of coffee. Then she quickly excused herself to fold some laundry. Okay, I thought, here it comes. The moment has arrived. I sat quietly lapping up the last bit of spaghetti sauce with my bread. He didn't say anything. He just sat there sipping his coffee. I thought about asking to be excused but decided, why wait for the inevitable?

"Daddy, did you take my silver dollars?"

"Yes," he said looking over his coffee cup.

"Why?"

"I needed them. Something came up. But don't worry I will replace them. You'll get them back. Look, Ricky, times have been a little tough lately. I need you to understand."

I felt like I had been hit in the stomach. The worst of what I had anticipated had come true.

"Dad, I loved those silver dollars. Each one was special to me."

"Now you are being a bit ridiculous," he snapped. "I said I would replace them." He took a sip of coffee and waited for my reply.

I had no strength to respond. I knew it was not going to change things anyway. If I had gone into a litany of reasons why those mint marks were special, it would have only angered him more. I desperately needed to leave the room. Any second I knew I was going to cry. I put on my best face.

"I understand. You're right. Can I be excused?"

"Okay. But listen, I am going to replace them. You understand that, right?"

"Yes sir. I understand." I replied with a polite smile and the only strength I could muster. I tried to look under control as walked passed Mom into my room. I gently closed the door, turned on the radio, put my head into my pillow and bawled.

I was devastated and angry. I swore I would never forgive him. For him to have taken those dollars and taken them without asking me, I thought crossed every line of trust we had between us. I was right and he was wrong. It was as simple as that.

That should have been my first clue. With right and wrong, nothing is that simple, especially not when people and relationships are involved and particularly when mercy and wisdom should be guiding principles.

Perhaps if I had read the book "The Yearling" or something like it and been touched with life's "bigger picture," I would have chosen a different way of dealing with my anger. Unfortunately, I didn't even know those options existed. There was nothing in my experience to calibrate or temper my thinking. Thus, my relationship with my father continued, but mostly on a superficial basis. The pain of that day led me to keep him at a distance. I put up a wall between us and left it there for protection. That decision exacted its own price, for nothing…is that simple.

Mom died in 1984 at the age of 67. She was very sick her last few years. Dad had to take care of her and do all the chores, including things he had never done: cooking, cleaning and the wash. When she died, he went from a man "in control" to a man "out of control." He struggled desperately with loneliness. He hated to have to return home at night from work or from whatever restaurant he had stopped at for dinner. He said it was simply too painful. I can remember several nights convincing him he had to go home.

His life had changed and he could barely keep up with it. Our relationship changed too. He went from a "handshake" type of guy to a real "hugger." He started calling me more often and sharing intimate details of his life. I wrestled with coming to grips with the "new Dad." I didn't know how to embrace this radical transition. Nevertheless, we began developing a whole new relationship. In three short years, I grew to love the change…and love him. It was a father son Renaissance which erased many bad memories and replaced them with spectacular ones.

I purposely chose the words, three short years, because that's what they were. I remember his call as if it was yesterday. It was mid-morning when he called on that early October day in 1987. I was in my office at home.

"Hey Ricky." I could hear a funny sound to his voice. I knew my father's vocal tones and this was the one which spoke of trouble.

"Hey Daddy, what's up?"

"I called to let you know that I had a medical test today. They spotted a tiny bit of cancer in my esophagus about the size of a pencil eraser."

I was stunned and couldn't find any words to respond. After a few seconds, I shook the shock, refocused, and tenderly requested "How serious is it?"

"They think if they operate immediately they can get all of it." I told my doctor to schedule it as soon as possible."

"How can I help?"

"Just hope all goes well." That was Daddy, never wanting to be an imposition to anyone, even his sons.

"Don't be silly. I want to be with you."

"There really isn't any need. Just pray all goes well," Daddy offered in a noticeably disguised tenor of voice.

"Like it or not, I am coming. When is your surgery?"

"Next Monday. If you are coming, I would rather you come after the surgery. Give me a chance to get out of the hospital and get back home. That's when I'll need the most help."

"Okay. I'll start making arrangements."

"Great. I look forward to seeing you.

"Me too Dad. See you soon." I didn't want him to hear the fear I felt inside. I hung up the phone with flashes of my mother's last days and her battle with cancer. They were the last thoughts I wanted to have creep into my consciousness.

Losing your first parent is very, very painful. The possibility of losing your second is doubly devastating. You taste for the first time what it will feel like to become an orphan. It consumed my thoughts. I hoped beyond hope that this was not the beginning of the end.

He called me the day of the surgery. I was working out of our house and surprised to get his call. He said he was in the hospital and soon to be taken down for the operation. Then he said, "I want to be serious for a moment." I responded with a gulp and an "uh oh." I felt my voice chocking up a bit. "You know Dad we have always kept things pretty light hearted. I'm not sure I know how to get real serious."

"Well, today needs to be. You know I have a bad heart." Dad had had several congestive heart failure attacks but hadn't had one recently. He continued, "There's a chance I won't survive the surgery. I couldn't go into today's operation without telling you that you have been a great son. I am so proud of you. I want you to know that I love you." His tone was the most compassionate tone he had ever spoken to me.

I didn't know what to say. I was overwhelmed and silent.

"Do you hear me?"

"Yes sir," I replied trying to hold back my tears. I knew I had to get control of myself and said bravely, "Look, I will be there in a couple of weeks. We will be having steak and beer in the kitchen! You're going to do fine. Dad, I love you too. You are a great father."

As hard as it is to believe, the second I said "You are a great father" and hung up the phone, the day of the forty nine silver dollars popped into my mind. What a fool I had been! I regretted not letting them go a long time ago. Many, many moments of when my father had been there for me, both visibly and behind the scenes, began to "weigh in" on my thinking. The parade of memories was humbling. He was a great father. He was not without imperfections; but I could easily say that about myself. God help the man who thinks he has not made mistakes.

To have secretly stewed over a few silver dollars in view of the Herculean efforts he made to keep our family afloat, was terribly, terribly wrong. I realized far too late that he must have had a very serious reason to have taken them. Perhaps they went for rent or maybe for groceries. Whatever it was, I regret that I had not given him the benefit of the doubt. What he had taken from me was monetarily insignificant. What he had given me, instilled in me, those life saving lessons of how to survive from one day to the next were priceless. All in all, it was one of those painful lessons at "Copernicus University." The kind where you learn you are not the center of the universe. I regret to say I have not yet passed the final exam.

Dad was forever in his own way trying to teach me the way to be there for other people. Sadly, I did not quickly grasp the subtleties of his wisdom. One of my dear friends, Nancy, related to me a similar story about her childhood that touches on the essence of the issue. She explains that for years her mom would bring the dinner to the table. Her father would say "Mom gets first choice." Her mother would always choose the "burnt pork chop" even when it was obvious that there were better ones on the serving plate. Nancy said for years she would giggle under her breath how foolish her mother was. After all, anyone could plainly see that it was the worst choice. Nancy says that she laughed for years until one day it dawned on her why her mother was always choosing the worst. She wanted her family to have the best. It was one of the subtle ways she could say "I love you" in addition to many others.

My Dad came out of the same mold. He rarely ever thought of himself first. His problem was how to please "his whole family." He had his immediate family and he had his extended family: a mother, five brothers, and two sisters. As a father to both, he was pulled in a thousand directions. How he dealt with the financial demands alone, never divulging the fear he must have faced daily of not having enough money to pay all the bills, spoke volumes about his character, integrity, and internal constitution. He never burdened anyone with this load; it was his way of expressing love. He bore it all. I couldn't wait to get home to be with him. I wanted to tell him what a giant of a man I thought he was and hug him like I hadn't done in a long while.

Dad survived the surgery but lost his battle in intensive care. His heart gave out after a two week struggle. I never got a chance to talk with him. His call that morning before his surgery was our last conversation.

If there was an epitaph to be written for my father, it would have been... "He was not blessed with riches, but he gave to others as if he had plenty."

Amazingly, after his death he left one last gift. He had secretly somewhere along the way "squirreled away" money for two investment retirement accounts: $2000 each for my brother and me. How he saved one penny on his income is a question for the ages. Nevertheless, I took it as his way of giving me a chance to get the silver dollars back and more.

I have never found any need to replace them. What I have found is the need to live and pass on his epitaph.

The Heart of the Matter

*"All things are filled full of signs, and it is a wise man
who can learn about one thing from another."*

Enneads, II, iii, 8
Plotinus. 205-270

There were signs, hundreds of them of every shape, color, and type. They were there when I woke up in the morning and there when I finally closed my eyes at night. There were some that would not leave and followed me into my dreams.

Looking back and reflecting on many of my experiences, it wasn't difficult to recognize some of the obvious "life-signs" that passed my way. In some form or fashion, there were many "Stop, Dead End, Speed Limit, Detour," as well as the "Thou shalt not" signs. For someone who seemingly had a predisposition for testing the rationale and limits for rules and authority, they were amazingly ubiquitous, easy to identify, and very direct in their message.

However, on the other end of the continuum, far more subtle and less conspicuous were the haunting "Is this all there is to life?" signs. They were more abstract, further off the side of the road, and far less frequent. Nevertheless, their timing was impeccable. They always seemed to know when to show up. Not so surprisingly, it was directly proportional to the level of futility and the emptiness I was feeling in my circumstances. I would like to say it was rooted in the frustration of not having many choices; choices about churches, schools, and whether or not to wear uniforms, but that would not be the truth. It was much deeper than that. I wanted to be connected with something larger than my circumstances; something that would offer hope rather than the fatalistic perspective, "well, that's life." Not having that connection, I struggled to know what to do with them. Too often I retreated to the clamor of family living hoping it would distract me enough to erase the troubling challenge that kept rearing its ugly head and resurfacing over and over again in my mind.

I grew up in a large Irish – Italian family; that, in itself, should speak volumes in terms of distractions. Stimulating the senses and elevating emotions was as fundamental as eating pasta or corned beef and cabbage. The Irish side in particular, with their innate love of parties, knew how to ratchet up the level of stimulation. They could throw together a party in a matter of moments. All it took was a chance meeting between a few, and then quick phone calls to the rest. It was amazing to me to observe, in the span of an evening, singing, dancing, and riotous laughter mixed with debates, diatribes and, regrettably on rare occasions, physical violence, all fueled by too much alcohol. Who needed television? It was live theatre, often of the bizarre.

One night, I watched one of my aunts, responding in a fit of anger to an indiscreet remark, fill a one quart saucepan with cold water which she intended to throw on her inebriated husband. The pot slipped out of her hand as she threw the water and hit my uncle square in the forehead. It knocked him out cold. He, being six foot four inches tall and two hundred and seventy pounds, fell over like a redwood. The sound when he hit the floor was like a two hundred and seventy five pound sack of potatoes being hurled off the upstairs balcony onto the wood floor below. She immediately leaned over his prostrate body to make sure he was still breathing and not bleeding. Once she had confirmed he was "okay," she began to chastise him for being a drunk and getting what he deserved.

The McDonoughs, my mother's side of the family, were not a clan for the faint at heart. They thrived on stimulation. It seemed to energize every part of their being. If the Catholic Church would have allowed, they would have canonized a new Saint, Saint Stimulation, and given her a feast day. It would have given them another reason to "Eat, drink, and be merry…and duck every once in a while."

Growing up, it was easy to be entertained and consumed by their feisty walk on the wild side. The crescendos of family clamor proved the perfect diversion for those moments when those thought provoking "life signs" stepped into view.

None the less it didn't take long to realize that the distractions were only a temporary remedy. The different forms of stimulation, which early on anesthetized the hollow feelings, began to lose their potency. I started to fill in the gaps with my own brand of drama. From my sophomore year in high school through my sophomore year in college, I deliberately chose a circle of friends who were open to pushing the limits of uncharted territory. Yet no matter how hard I tried, I couldn't eliminate the frustration and desperation that was building up inside of me.

There was something missing. I could feel it, but I couldn't identify it.

The quote from Plotinus at the onset of this chapter speaks about a wise man recognizing signs, learning one thing from another. I have never held any misconceptions about being wise. Most of my learning has come from making mistakes. I found out what was right by experiencing first what I had done wrong. I don't think that was exactly what Plotinus was insinuating. I wish I had been more adept at sensing some of the signs; it would have saved me from a great deal of wandering and poor choices.

Geoffrey Chaucer, the famous English poet and author of the <u>Canterbury Tales</u>, wrote in The Nun's Priest Tale the admonition: "Be wise, keep the grain but leave the chaff." For a long, long time I never could learn to leave the chaff alone. I unwisely thought of it as tasty as the grain. This was certainly one of the poorer choices I made and contributed to my learning and relearning the age old adage: there never has been, and will never be, a free lunch.

Nevertheless, even with some of the poor choices, I started to define what was missing, not by discerning what it might be, but by experiencing what it wasn't.

I resigned myself to this pseudo-Edison approach. Thomas Edison and his team went through well over a thousand materials before they came upon the perfect filament for the incandescent bulb. I concluded that my desire to find out the answer to the question, "Is this all there is to life," would take the same kind of effort. It wasn't going to come quickly. It would be a journey, full of emotional peaks and valleys, calling me out of the security of my surroundings. It has been all of that and more.

I will share this insight. While on the surface experiences seem random and disconnected, I am convinced that they are not. Each one is inextricably linked with the one before and the one after, however convoluted it might seem in our own understanding. Each is a part of a deliberate pathway pointing clearly to an answer or the answer. I believe that our mission in life is to find that answer. Along the way we must be mindful to recognize the distractions for what they are, resist their disabling capacities, rise above the clamor, seek out the substance that touches our soul, and claim the purpose for which we are created.

Part Two:
Encouraging Hands

Teachers

Like giant rocks in the river of life, they play a vital role in helping the river reach its destination. They channel these torrents, these boundless amounts of energy, these unshaped lives which briefly pass their doorway to consider the many paths of opportunity that exist, and journey beyond.

They have the tender touch of a Potter.

They hold in their hands the emerging minds of tomorrow. They honor this privilege with all that they are. In every soul they see the potential of a Mozart, a Michelangelo, a Milton, a Van Gogh, a Pasteur, and a Kierkegaard waiting to be lifted up. They meticulously mold, gently guide, and hold steady these new forms rising out of the clay.

They have the eyes of a Sculptor.

They peer into the mass of stone and recognize what needs to be set free. With their mallet and chisel they patiently chip away on the constraining outer layers always mindful of the final goal. They are undeterred, tenderly relentless, and creative.

They have the heart of a missionary.

They understand the depth and meaning of the word sacrifice. It rests in the core of their being and inspires them to serve. They recognize that some will hear and others will choose not to. Some will come close while others will keep their distance. Still others may not even care. No matter, they persist. They are not driven by numbers; they are driven by a faith and belief that extends far beyond human formulas.

They are heroes of the first order who try to give above and beyond the call of duty every single day. They love to build lives, to change lives, and to send them on their way.

I wish this was a commentary on every teacher I ever had, but regrettably, it only pertains to a special few. I consider myself blessed to have known them. Their passion for connecting their subject matter to the realities of life completely captured my attention and often left me not wanting to breathe so as not to miss a single word. They aroused in me values which far exceeded the mechanics of the classroom. Yet in those mechanics they not only gave me the tools to define the emotions and the recollections that were stirring in my soul but also laid out the many avenues that were available to express them. I chose what felt most comfortable, to frame them with words.

John Keats wrote in his poem *Sleep and Poetry*, "O for ten years, that I might overwhelm myself in poesy; so I may do the deed that my own soul has to itself decreed." The moment I read those words and heard my professor render them with sincerity, something in my soul nodded in agreement. It was a sense of realizing a purpose for the first time. It confirmed why I loved to write, why I loved to paint pictures with a broad pallet of words.

It was something that had been decreed. I was supposed to write them down and pass them on. It crystallized in my mind that each of us is assigned many purposes in life. It is our duty to try to fulfill them with whatever we have been given.

I remember coming to that realization. I remember wanting to thank "the rocks" who had wisely and unselfishly led me to it. However, the time to do that had long passed. The river is ever moving and, though we may rest in an eddy on occasion, we are never still. We can only look back and praise them at a distance.

Mona Lisa

*"Discovery consists of seeing what everybody has seen
and thinking what nobody has thought."*

From I.J. Good, *The Scientist Speculates*
Albert Szent-Gyorgyi von Nagyrapolt. 1962

I loved Mother Chrysostom. She was a tall Benedictine nun traditionally dressed in a black gown, a black and white habit, which framed her face in sort of a triangle, and with a silver cross pendant hanging from her neck. She was a beacon of encouragement for me at St. Bridget's Catholic School as she was someone who knew the value of truth and how to get you to embrace it. It was radiant in her countenance. She had penetrating eyes, expressive eyebrows, and a disarming smile. I had such respect for her. I believe that every teacher you have leaves you with something to remember. Mother Chrysostom left me with a new appreciation for truth and the power of words. Words can be illuminating. Words can be provocative.

It was just another day of waiting to find out what grade I had received on a composition. Mother Chrysostom had collected them a few days before and this day had decided to read a few of them to the class. It was early December and the assignment had been broad: Write about Christmas. I don't recall the first few she read, however, the last one still sticks in my mind. Steve Larsen, a fellow student, had written about a Christmas parade of the future. It featured two television announcers commenting on the garish floats passing their main viewing stands. With each spectacular description, I found myself tuning in more and more and letting go of my normal mid-morning distractions which mostly centered on what the hot lunch would be in the cafeteria and who would be on the kickball teams at recess. Cascading forward like dominoes, the whole class began leaning forward in their desks as Steve's words worked their imagination into a listening frenzy. The next to last float was an outlandish portrayal of a chubby space-helmeted Santa about to climb into a space capsule outlined in green neon lights, perched on top of a 30 foot gleaming white and blue striped colored rocket. Rudolf too, red nose blinking and antlers, was space suit clad and about to climb into the other side. Mother Chrysostom kept a serious look on her face. She kept on reading: "And finally here comes the last float. Let's see what it is. With all the fantastic looks into the future, what could culminate this marvelous parade? I can see it now. There is a bright star high in the air on the front of it. It is the....Baby Jesus? What in the world does the Baby Jesus scene have to do with the future? Isn't he a bit out of date for where we are headed today? I am afraid the parade organizers have missed the mark here. What a disappointment! No doubt many will be offended with this decision. Look at the disgusted looks on some of the faces in the crowd. What in the world were the organizers thinking? Makes you wonder what will happen next year. Well, we hate to leave you on such a controversial note but we have to return you to your local channel. Good night, ladies and gentlemen. Hope you have a happy holiday, prosperous New Year and...oh yes...Merry Christmas."

I am sure I don't remember the exact words of the composition. However, I do remember the distinct feelings that began churning in my heart. I remember the powerful silence that came after Mother Chrysostom finished. While still staring at the paper she commented softly..."written by Steve Larsen." Mixed emotions simultaneously collided in my mind. I remember wanting to clap, but clapping didn't seem the cool thing to do. Being cool plays an enormous filtering role in eighth grade. So quietly in my mind, my soul yelled out, "Way to go Steve," and I looked around the room to see if any other faces were reflecting similar thoughts, especially Mother Chrysostom. She just looked pensive and began to scan the room with her eyes. Then someone broke the tension with a clap. That was all I needed. My hands impulsively added to the rising tide of clamor. They started to sting as I clapped vigorously harder and harder. I was not cheering any theological statement. I was applauding the dramatic ending that had opened my eyes much like a blind man seeing things for the first time or opening a Christmas present to find something totally unexpected that in the first few moments leaves you breathless. Concurrently, and equally sobering, was the feeling of distance. Nothing like this had ever crossed my mind. The gap between our abilities was obvious and cavernous. I was laboring to construct sentences, fussing with grammar and syntax...finger-painting...while he used words like brushstrokes.... acrylics, oils, or better said, pen and ink on a much different canvass.

Mother Chrysostom knew what she was doing. I don't know if Steve Larsen ever thought about it. There was a simple truth that day. She was carefully and wisely planting seeds. She knew if she could stand her students in front of an eighth grade "Mona Lisa," finger-painting would never be the same. It worked on me. From that day onward, Steve Larsen got more of my respect; Mother Chrysostom got more of my heart, and, for the first time in my life, words began a voyage from their dictionary homeland of functionality to an unexplored new world of inspiration.

SHUMATE, CLEMENT, DANCY, AND JOHNSON

"So long as men can breathe, or eyes can see,
So long lives this, and this gives life to thee."

Sonnet 18.Verses 13-14
William Shakespeare. 1564-1616

No, this is not the name of a law firm who helped me get out of a few brushes with the constabulary; although there were moments when one might have been handy. These are the names of four teachers who in my Junior and Senior years of high school were instrumental in encouraging me to take my first steps at putting my thoughts on paper.

Miss Margaret F. Shumate, graduate of Longwood College, was a member of the business faculty that instructed preparatory classes at Hermitage High School. Petite in stature, five feet four inches tall, she was an attractive woman with short flipped blond hair and charismatic smile. Always smartly dressed, she was an intelligent dynamo whose business acumen, leadership, and motivational skills would have well suited her to have been a corporate CEO. When she walked into a room, she took command. She was a woman with vision and a mission. Every class was a "buckle your safety belt" type of an adventure. She was demanding, opinionated, unrelenting, and captivating. So captivating, I don't remember anyone in our class who didn't want to pay the price of admission: punctuality, completed homework, focus, and an open mind. Sitting in her class was a privilege. When Ms. Shumate paid you a compliment, it stuck to your bones. It was accurate, to the point, and well thought out. It stayed with you for days and became the fuel for future performance.

The accounting knowledge, and all the attendant bookkeeping skills I learned in her class, had far reaching effects on my career. It didn't have an auspicious beginning. When I signed up for the course, some of my friends chastised me saying, "It was a class for 'those' who were not planning on going to college." I was shaken and began thinking I had inadvertently closed a very important door. No statement could have been further from the truth. Not only did it prepare me for college, it opened my eyes to possibilities beyond arts and humanities, such as Corporate Finance, Business Administration, and Law.

Even after getting my undergraduate degree, it helped me, in my first job, to get the top grade in an evening business course I took at a local university. My professor commented, "You should be proud of this. You beat out a number of students who are Accountants. Where in the world does a Human Resource Manager learn some of the intricacies of closing the books you demonstrated on your final exam?"

"You should have known Margaret Shumate," came easily out of my mouth.

In addition to the Principles of Accounting, Ms. Shumate also taught Business English. It was here she opened another amazing door for me. One of the early homework assignments was to keep a journal for thirty days. "Write whatever comes to your mind," she instructed. "Don't be too concerned about punctuation or structure; just try to get your thoughts into words and on paper. We will tackle syntax a little later."

I struggled. Everything I thought about seemed too mundane. I wrote about basketball, football, intramural sports, coin collecting, and running. One day, during a quiet writing moment in class, a guy two desks behind me raised his hand. Ms. Shumate went to him and began talking in a low whisper. I could hear them. He said he had written a song and wanted her opinion. A song, I thought. As they began talking about rhythm and meter, my heart sank. Nothing like that had crossed my mind. I leaned over to a friend sitting next to me and whispered, "Did you hear that? Jeff is writing songs." Carol remarked, "He has a band. They like to play their own material." I heard what she said but I couldn't get any words to come out of my mouth. I was trying to come to grips with the thought. Carol had a tender heart and could read the dismay, the feeling of inadequacy on my face. "Songs are just poems," she said with a look of compassion. I know you could write poems."

"You of all people could write poems, Mr. Baldacci," Ms. Shumate whispered, leaning close to my ear. I quickly turned around in surprise that she had picked up on our conversation. She had finished with Jeff and was returning to the front of the room. "There is a lot going on in that mind of yours. I see it on your face everyday. I can't wait to read how you choose to describe those thoughts."

"Thank you," Ms. Shumate. "I can't tell you how much that means to me." I wanted to say more but was overwhelmed with her encouragement. She patted me on the shoulder and returned to her desk. "Hey, I want to read them too," Carol remarked. I just smiled and nodded my head.

In Caesar's Gallic Wars, he describes a battle where his men were faltering. He rode from the top of the hill where he was overlooking the skirmish, dismounted, and ran close to the front lines. He began calling out the names of the men. When the men on the front line heard his encouraging voice, the very voice of Julius Caesar calling their individual names, they rallied themselves and went on to win the day.

Miss Sandra L. Clements, graduate from Longwood College, served as a member of the History Department, and also served as the "Sponsor" for The Scroll, the school's literary magazine, featuring works by members of the Hermitage student body. There were collections of poems, essays, and short stories, some written for class assignments and others for pleasure. She taught U.S. History in such a way that it left an indelible impression.

In many ways Ms. Clement was the antithesis of Ms. Shumate. She was taller, had brunette hair which she always curled into a bun and rarely wore makeup. She wasn't as meticulous about her appearance nor was she anywhere near being as adept with her organization skills. Where Ms. Shumate had everything on her desk perfectly in order, Ms. Clement regularly came to class and threw files and books on her desk, not seemingly worried in the least about any method of arrangement. Ms. Shumate was conservative, directed, on course at all times, whereas Ms. Clement was liberal, fluid, and "earthy." She had that "Bette Midler" swagger about herself. She could take dry historical facts and turn them into tantalizing, sensuous, melodramas. Every day was a "One Act Play" you didn't want to miss. Her embellished descriptions of historical events often evoked applause from the class. Yet in all of the hoopla and Hollywood atmosphere, there was a shrewdness emanating from Ms. Clements. You couldn't see it but you could definitely feel it. The subliminal message was as powerful as her performance. She loved history and was determined to transfer its importance and its ramifications straight from the page to the forum of your mind. It had a resounding effect on me. To this day I cannot stop picking up books about historical events or the biographies of famous people who have changed the course of their time. The history channel is my first stop on television and "the yellow pie" is always the first I go after when playing the game Trivial Pursuit. It is a living tribute to a woman who had passion, and with great finesse, knew how to give it away.

Like Ms. Shumate, Ms. Clement was a "door opener." One day in class she suggested that I join her in working on The Scroll. She said, "You have some promise in that pen of yours. Why don't you come down this afternoon to The Scroll office and help me read some of the thoughts of your fellow students? It might give you a few things to think about." I was honored that she would even ask. It proved to be one of those afternoons I would remember for a lifetime.

"Well, what do you think?" She asked with a glint in her eye.

"I had no idea, no idea anything like this quality of writing was going on. A lot of these poems, essays, and stories are outstanding. Nancy Murdock's 'These are the eyes of war' poem left me stunned. What a moving description of the faces on the casualties of war!"

"Yes, that poem will make the publication this semester. Nancy is a gifted writer."

"I won't be able to look at Nancy the same way anymore. There is a part of me that just wants to shake her hand and say thank you for having the courage to share such powerful words."

"What's stopping you? You know she is a member of The Scroll staff, don't you? If you joined the team you would get a chance to work with her everyday. You would have plenty of time to work up the courage".

"I would feel like a little leaguer trying to play with the New York Yankees."

"I think Mickey Mantle started out as a bat boy," she retorted. "Besides, think of the stimulation of just being in Yankee Stadium!"

Ms. Clement leaned forward at her desk and got an impassioned look on her face. "Think about the opportunity to interact with people who share

80

the same passion for writing as you do. Think about what James Madison must have felt writing the Federalist Papers with John Jay and Alexander Hamilton."

Ms. Clement stared at me for a moment and then flashed a big smile, recognizing she had fallen back into her passion.

"Your love of history is inspiring," I said.

"Your love for writing is inspiring," She countered putting her hand on my shoulder. "Will I see you here tomorrow?"

"Yes, you will." I offered my handshake as confirmation. "With a lot of butterflies in my stomach."

"Butterflies? Where would we be if Admiral Farragut had taken that attitude in the War Between the States? We could still be whistling Dixie right now." She raised her fist in vehemence. "Liberty and union, now and forever, one and inseparable. Let's give a big hand to Daniel Webster!"

"See you tomorrow, Ms. Clement," I said shaking my head at her obsession as I walked out of the room. She waved and gave me the thumbs up sign of approval.

It was another page turning day. The kind of a day when you knew that tomorrow would truly begin another chapter in your life. Ms. Shumate had carefully put the thought of writing in my mind. Ms. Clement had strapped me onto the saddle and whacked the end of my horse!

Ms. Marilyn M. Dancy, graduate of Westhampton College, was a member of the English Department. She was tall, at least five ten, with short curly blonde hair. She had larger than normal blue eyes and a prim and proper, manicured mystique. She often dressed in Edwardian puffed sleeved blouses, long plaid scarves, capes and hats of all sorts. She projected a real sense of class. I always imagined she would have made the perfect wife for Alfred Lord Tennyson.

When she entered a room, you immediately felt the need to stand up, or at least sit up straight. She evoked manners out of everyone. I remember how quickly she could switch from a disarming smirk to a penetrating cold stare.

She was my senior English Literature teacher. The year was filled with reading a variety of poetry, Sir Walter Scott's <u>Ivanhoe</u>, and Shakespeare's <u>Macbeth</u>. It was also filled with quite a bit of extemporaneous writing and a lengthy term paper. Ms. Dancy constantly challenged us to examine the context of each piece, the perspective of the author, themes, the direction of the plot and subplots, and more often, how the character fulfilled his or her purpose. She was firmly committed to make you look beyond the obvious. Her watchwords were: think, analyze, scrutinize, probe, investigate, reconnoiter, inspect; and then with the same amount of dedication: characterize, develop, organize, and support your findings with well thought out ideas and carefully chosen words.

Her class standards were rigorous and unrelenting. She regularly questioned phrases and words on test papers, but never in a demeaning way. This was her genius. She not only knew how to communicate the power of words but she also knew how to constructively stimulate and mold that same desire for excellence in you. Getting a good grade in her class made you exuberant and fiercely loyal.

I was utterly spent at the end of the year and profoundly grateful. We had covered a lot of ground. I remember sitting in the last class of the year, chatting with two of my friends. We were congratulating each other on finishing strong and making the grade. "After this year, English Literature 101 at the University of Richmond should be a breeze," my friend Sharon said snapping her fingers. "Yes, if we can get through this," another friend Richard chimed in, "we can get through anything!"

I knew Ms. Dancy heard Richard's remark. He was never accused of having a soft voice or decorum. I quickly looked to the front of the room and caught her eye. She flashed that infamous smirk on her face as she pretended not to be bothered by his comment. Then her smirk faded into a more pensive stare. Her moment of reflection spurred one in me.

What came out of my heart were appreciation and a view of her in a different light. She had taken a rag-tag bunch of "space cadets," shaken a little reality into us, laid out an aggressive game plan, and never compromised her principles. All along she knew the type of cadence it would take to make the finish line for the year and she also knew what kind of foundation it would take for us to be prepared for future finish lines. With a mindset similar to a cross between drill sergeant and that of a physical therapist, she relentlessly made us flex our minds and our writing muscles. Lessening the load, would have bordered on malfeasance. She would never have let herself even consider it. She concentrated on strengthening, on acuity, on giving us a fighting chance toward facing the inevitable demands that she knew were just over the horizon.

As I stared at her, I began comprehending the enormity of the value of the gift she had so unselfishly given to us. The final bell of the final class rang. I got up walked to her desk held out my hand to say thank you. Ms. Dancy, ever true to her nature, grabbed mine and gave me a firm handshake while offering an admonition: "I expect great things out of you, Mr. Baldacci. Remember, if you want something bad enough, you must be prepared to work very, very hard for it."

I responded with the truth that was stirring inside of my soul, "Believe me; I certainly understand that lesson more than I did a year ago. The test will be if I can discipline myself enough so as to make it a part of me." I stared at her for a moment, smiled, and said, remembering a line from Shakespeare's Macbeth, "Then tomorrow won't creep in its petty pace from day to day, to the last syllable of recorded time."

Always quick with her rapier wit, she retorted from the same Act: "And it won't be a tale told by an idiot, full of sound and fury, signifying nothing!"

"I am going to miss you," I lamented.

"Yes, you will," she said with her ever present effervescent smile. She then donned her beret, scarf and shawl, gave me a feisty wink, a soft punch on my upper arm and walked out of the room with a swagger that defined the unique character she was.

And from that day, she has been right.

Robert L. Johnson, graduate of William and Mary College, was a member of the History department. He also enjoyed key sponsorship roles in Dramatic Arts, Hermitage Players, and Audio Visual Aids. Mr. Johnson stood five foot ten, had trimmed wavy white hair, dark black glasses, and a long loping gait much like that of Groucho Marx. Students were forever mimicking his "walk" behind him in the halls. He had a sharp tenor voice which could be heard in the next county. He was enigmatic, idiosyncratic, annoying, funny, giving, keenly observant, talented, and extremely intelligent. He was definitely not someone whose personality and interests you could put in one box. He was a collage of many, a gifted jack of all trades.

He taught Government classes for all seniors. He arranged a most interesting curriculum. The first half of the first semester was directed at learning not only how Congress makes laws but also the rules of order for conduct within the House of Representatives. Then the second half of the first semester, all seniors met in the auditorium as members of the House. Each senior was given a State to represent. I was the senior member of the State of Arkansas delegation. Each of us was assigned a committee from which to propose a law for debate in front of the whole assembly and ultimately have it taken to final vote.

One would think that 435 seniors congregated in an auditorium for two hours would have been a recipe for mayhem. To the contrary, Mr. Johnson drove the "House" operations with the same steeled determination and tenacity that would have made a Sam Rayburn, Lyndon Johnson, or "Tip" O'Neal proud. You never knew when he would scream out, "Point of order, Mr. Chairman" or "Point of Personal Privilege" and commence to confront students not focused on the issues at hand. His knowledge of your State's commerce, activity, and history was simply amazing. He did his homework and set the standard for everyone else to follow. Getting caught in a debate with him without being prepared was embarrassing.

In addition to his prowess within the classroom, Mr. Johnson directed many school plays and trained a variety of students to support the needs of the school with the ever changing world of audio visual aids equipment. He was a complex individual whose selfless efforts reached into every corner of school life. I could not fathom the number of hours he must have worked above and beyond the call of duty.

That thought alone made me hold him in awe. However, one spring afternoon he raised my appreciation even higher.

We were having our final test on the three branches of government, covering a number of essay questions as well as a long list of definitions. I wrote furiously responding to the essay questions and gave special attention to the definitions, one in particular. The word was populace. When I came to it, I rolled my eyes thinking that could be a paper all to itself. After serious deliberation, it struck me what to write: "The people; we who elect." It was one of those moments of inspiration. I wondered what Mr. Johnson would think. Was it too flippant? Was it just a moment of insanity? I decided to go with my heart and leave it exactly as I wrote it. After all, the words, we who elect, not only defined the role but also communicated the quintessential power of the populace.

A couple of weeks later Mr. Johnson was reviewing the test with the class. "I had one hundred and fifty odd tests to read over five classes. Now let's get to this class' answers." Methodically he went through every essay question and definition. When he came to the word populace, he paused. He stared off into the distance for a few seconds and then looking deliberately around the classroom, stopped when his eyes hit my face. For a moment I thought I was in for some trouble. Perhaps he hated my answer and was going to make his point at my expense. I froze in place and braced for the worst. I immediately started second guessing my decision to go with my heart. Then he broke his silence and said compassionately, "Mr. Baldacci, I really liked your answer. It was succinct and eloquent. Would you read it to the class?" I was stunned by his remark. I read it aloud to the class. He made me read it twice more. "Thank you, Mr. Baldacci. You have a gift for words." After a few seconds of staring down at his desk, he moved on to the next test answer. Inwardly, I was elated with his encouragement and wanting to cry at the same time at the emotional relief of having stuck with my instincts. The fact that he had identified with the emotion that I had felt when writing the words also left me reeling. Outwardly, I just quickly smiled at the students sitting near me and then pretended to refocus on the test.

In the whole scope of things, it was a simple moment between a teacher and a student. Yet in that simple moment Mr. Johnson, deluged with the ever growing demands on his time, had not allowed those demands to trample on the little glimmer of joy he found in a few carefully chosen words and the student who had put his heart into them.

SPELLBOUND

"I can scarcely bid you goodbye, even in a letter."

From his last letter
John Keats.1821

She had the look of an English Literature professor but the feel of an easy chair. She had short brown hair, rosy cheeks, a delicate physique, engaging smile, and a relaxed easy going aura. Her inviting blue eyes made you comfortable the minute you met her.

When Ms. Stevenson read poetry she left you spellbound. Her command of inflection, phrasing, and pause for effect was mesmerizing. It was if iambic pentameter was her first language. She had the unique ability to take words off the page, reach into your heart, and ring the doorbell of your soul. Her gift was revival. She could not only make words come alive but she could make them influence. Days in her sophomore class were exhilarating, emotional, and exhausting at the same time.

What I most remember about her was her love of John Keats. She read "The Eve of St. Agnes," "Sleep and Poetry," "Ode to a Grecian Urn," "Ode to a Nightingale," "Ode on Melancholy," "When I Have Fears," and "Adonais" with such passion, I felt like I was inside his thoughts. I knew what he was feeling with every stanza. A thousand emotions leapt into my mind and exploded, saturating my consciousness with volcanic amounts of pathos. I started feeling things I had never felt before; and what's more, I wanted to put them on paper. Wherever I was, I would stop and quickly scribble out whatever thought or inspiration that kept echoing in my mind from a recent event. At times it was a necessity to stop and write because the thought would irrationally dominate every other thought until it was relegated to my pen. At times I felt like Vincent Van Gogh, growing crazier with each passing day.

Just when I thought I could not ingest any more stimulation, Ms. Stevenson gave a "tour de force" performance one warm afternoon in the spring semester. We had again returned to the work of John Keats but this time his letters. Ms. Stevenson's class met at 2:30 p.m. in a room facing the southwestern Virginia sun. Many of my friends had trouble staying awake after eating a big lunch and allowed the rising temperature to lull themselves into the "arms of Morpheus". The sandman, as every college student knows, carries a big stick in the early afternoon.

I might have fallen prey to the same malady if I hadn't taken notice of a different look on Ms. Stevenson's face when she entered the room. There was a somber look in her eyes. But true to her aplomb, she hid it well. She began the class with a discussion on the value of letters, their varied purposes, and their insight into the author's personality. She asked for examples of some of the best letters we had received and had us discuss why they were so meaningful.

After about a thirty minute discussion, we launched into some of Keats' letters. I studied her countenance because I began to sense some slight changes in her voice. She was calculatingly moving in a direction that began to set off every bell in my psyche. With about ten minutes to go in the class, she asked us to close our textbooks. She said she wanted to read the last letter John Keats ever wrote. She explained that he had contracted tuberculosis and had been persuaded to spend his last days in a milder climate than England. He and his friend Joseph Severn ventured to Rome, to a house that literally bordered the Spanish Steps. There, in what Keats called his "posthumous existence," he penned this letter to his friend, Charles Brown.

"Ask yourself," she said, "as I read, what you hear in these last words? Ask yourself some time in the next twenty four hours, if the same circumstances arose, what would you like to say in your last letter?" Then she began to read.

It is impossible to explain what transpired during the few minutes it took to listen as she read. What I remember is that she took on the persona of Keats himself. It was if she called up every emotion in her past and allowed it to fuel the tenor of her presentation. Every sentence had the powerful impact of a sledge hammer and the aroma of a crushed rose pedal. I remember the tears welling up in my eyes as she tenderly read the last lines: "I can scarcely bid you good-bye, even in a letter. I always made an awkward bow. God bless you! John Keats."

She gently closed her book, returned to that her far away look in her countenance, and said, "See you Thursday." She collected her books and made her way out of the door.

I was stunned. I felt like I had been hit by a tidal wave of emotion. I quickly collected myself and pretended to be making some notes as my buddies left. "I'll catch up with you in the cafeteria," I muttered not trying to give them any reason to stare at me. When the room was empty, I sat there quietly and reflected on what had happened.

It was another one of those page turning days. You know the kind; the kind, when your heart tells you that this day or this moment, is radically different than the norm and you are never going to be able to forget it; the kind, where you just have to stop, take a breath and pay homage to what has occurred in front of your eyes.

I was never able to look at Ms. Stevenson in the same way. My appreciation for her gifts reached reverential proportions. I knew that she saw the change in my countenance each time I looked at her. Every once in a while, throughout the end of the semester, she would give me a stare and a smile that transcended normal communication. Her message was unmistakable. Thank you for understanding what John Keats' work means to me.

The last class was difficult to leave. I don't remember one thing about what was discussed. I just remember staring at her and reminding myself how fortunate I had been to have experienced her teaching, her friendship, and the depth of feeling she was able to share in words.

THE MAN FROM WHEATLEY HILL

"Iron sharpens iron, so one man sharpens another."

Proverbs 27:17

It was a Friday night in the fall of 1984. I had just spent an exhausting week working at our Kensington office in west London, the European headquarters for our computer company. When the last meeting of the day ended, I grabbed my weekend bag and hailed a cab for the Kings Cross – St. Pancras train station. I had thought about jumping onto the Underground at High Street and taking the Central Line around, but I knew the moment I slid back into the soft tan leather seats of the shiny black English Ford I had made the right choice. The comfort, the quiet, and enjoying the sights of my favorite big city, helped me justify the expense. Besides, I didn't want to miss my train connection and London cabbies had a reputation for making good time. My decision proved correct as I arrived at the station with fifteen minutes to spare. I got into a short queue, purchased a return ticket to York, England, and made my way from the ticket lines through the crowds of crisscrossing commuters to my train. Getting out of the city and relaxing in the Yorkshire Moors seemed a much better option than staying in town and catching "the tube" to the flea markets just north of London in Camden Town Lock.

As I boarded the train, I was relieved that I had bought a reserved seat. The train was full. I actually got the last seat in my car. I stored my bag in the rack above the seats, and sat down. I couldn't wait to feel the train make its way out of the station and hear the melodious clicks and feel the occasional side to side movement which accompanied its speed along the tracks. I heaved a big sigh as I wondered why America had given up on this mode of travel. Not only did it make perfect economic sense from a mass transportation point of view, it was simply a lovely way to travel. Staring out the window, I waxed nostalgic thinking of the beautiful ambience this train station offered to travelers and the historical contribution it made to the character of this city of antiquities. I loved the high arcing ceilings and the echoing sounds of arrival and departure announcements. A slight jerk of movement brought me back to reality as I could feel the train moving. I looked down at my watch and thought a late dinner at my favorite Bed and Breakfast, Heworth Court owned by Janet Smith, would soon help wash away the turbulent trials of the past few weeks. The entrees and desserts that came out of her kitchen were epicurean delights. After dinner, I would try to grab a glass of port wine with her and her husband Terry in their Pub just off the dining room, and get an update on the latest happenings. They always kept me laughing with their hilarious stories. I was confident that Heworth Court was the perfect respite for a weary soul.

I leaned back in my seat and tried to decide whether a short nap was in order or whether I wanted to spend the time journaling. My journal won out. Since 1979, I have found it a compelling sanctuary for recording not only my travels and thoughts, but also the emotions behind them. Writing itself has always been cathartic for me. Amassing a personal history has proven to be its own therapeutic bonus, providing a means to look back and reflect on the many trials and blessings of my life. I reached up and pulled the heavy hard cover black and red book with its lined pages from my bag. I liked the style because it reminded me of the typical accounting books that once were a mainstay of the profession. It also gave me the feeling of being official, something duly noted in a proper place. With an overhead stretch of my arms, I was ready to make my next entry.

I had been writing for an hour when the gentleman sitting next to me on my left, caught me staring out the window, pensively trying to capture the next flood of words. He interrupted. "You seem to have a lot on your mind."

I was grateful for the interruption and turned my attention to him. "I do. However, tonight I don't seem to be able to find the right words to describe them."

"From the looks of your journal, you have given it a fair shot."

"Yes, I certainly got on a roll, didn't I?" I replied.

Gesturing with his hand, he said, "Don't let me stop you. I didn't mean to break your chain of thought."

"No, I am done for now. I will pick it up tomorrow." I closed my book. Where are you heading?"

"Darlington, I live there. I just came down for a conference and now I am heading home. How about you?"

"I work for a computer company in the States and we have a European Headquarters in Kensington, actually right across the street from Kensington Palace. I'm just over on a business trip for a couple of weeks. On the weekends I like to get out into the country. I'm heading for York to a favorite bed and breakfast. Tomorrow I can't wait to walk the walls, tour The Minster, and shop in the Shambles. On Sunday, I may even hire a car and drive through the Moors to Whitby. I love visiting the ruins of the Abby up on the hill."

"Yes, York is a beautiful town and the drive to Whitby is quite nice. Have you ever been to Harrowgate?" he asked.

"No," I responded. "Is it far from York?"

"Not at all," he countered. "It is a little more off the beaten path yet it has a real interesting charm of its own. It has a number of antique furniture stores if you are into that kind of thing. It's a place to go to relax, enjoy the beautiful gardens and not fight the crowds. My wife and I have spent some wonderful weekends there."

"I like off the beaten path kinds of places," I said exuberantly. "Harrowgate sounds like a very interesting option. I've been looking for a mantel clock or wall clock for my wife for her birthday."

"You'll have no problem finding one there," he said with authority.

Within in few minutes, what started as a northern England geography and tourism lesson quickly turned into open dialogue. For the next few hours the two of us covered a myriad of topics: English humor, American politics, healthcare, BBC News versus the American media, bird watching, sports, including golf, lawn bowling, fishing, hiking, and, of course, the laws of Cricket.

We moved in and out of subjects with ease. I remember particularly outlining some of the decisions my father faced relative to the healthcare of my mother during the last days of her life. He, being a doctor, was struck by the insensitivity of the life or death choices offered to him for my mother and shared his vision on how it might have been better handled. His words of wisdom poured much needed salve on some of the tender wounds that still lingered in my memory of her death. He shared some of his struggles with the National Health Service, how frustrating it was to work within the bureaucracy, and his ability to remain close to the patient. Our conversation reached levels that good friends don't reach for years. The level of kindred spirit and trust between us clicked on like a light bulb. There wasn't a gradual build up; it simply came on full force. For me, it was as if I had met a long lost brother and couldn't stop wanting to be caught up in his life.

I had completely forgotten all about my weekend plans. I was happily lost in conversation until the short brim capped, blue uniformed conductor made his way through the car, announcing in a loud voice, "York. Ten minutes. Next stop, York." It felt like he had come by and just turned off the video that I was engrossed in, right before its ending. I was very disappointed and could see the same frustration on my new friend's face.

"Well, unfortunately, this is where I get off." I reached for my bag in the overhead compartment.

"Darlington is thirty minutes further. That's my stop." Then, after a brief pause and a penetrating stare between us, he interjected, "I don't think we've finished this conversation, have we?"

"No, we haven't," I replied. "I wish we had more time."

"Do you have a business card with you?" he asked.

"A good Human Resource person always has a card." I said with a smile, handing him one from the front pocket of my shirt.

He quickly wrote down his personal information and handed it to me. Then he said, "When you are back this way, why don't you give me a ring. My wife and I would love to have you up for a restful weekend."

"I'm coming back to Britain on my regular business run in about a month. I'm going to take you up on that offer."

"Right then, we will expect you." He put out his hand to shake mine.

A month later on a Saturday morning, I wasn't sure what I expected when the train pulled into Darlington Station. Edwin was there waiting for me. It was an easy drive to his home in Sadberge, a small village on the outskirts of town. We pulled up in front of a two story brick farmhouse with a slate roof and a red front door. I couldn't wait to see the interior and the back yard. He informed me that the house was built in the late 1700's. He and his wife had hired a contractor to completely gut the insides, and on a frugal budget, had had it remodeled.

It was charming, every inch of it. There was a simple English country elegance that was captivating. I threw my bag in the upstairs bedroom and then found my way to one of the easy chairs in front of their fireplace. Edwin had already started a fire with clean burning coal.

"Well," he said, "what would you like to see and do while you're here?"

"Nothing." I answered as I stared at the fire in the fireplace.

"What do you mean?" he asked.

"Honestly, I really don't want to do anything that requires getting in a car or any other mode of transportation. Our company has been experiencing rough times. I have been laying off thousands of employees around the world. The process and the travel have been excruciating. I am weary and I would like to relax in front of your fireplace, enjoy your company, and continue that talk we started on the train. Let's sip on cups of tea, take a few walks, and let me treat you and Kim to some dinner tonight at the town pub we passed up the street. I think it was called "The Three Tuns."

Without missing a beat, he replied, "Nothing it is. You don't have to sell me on unwinding. Unwinding is near and dear to my heart as well. There's only one issue with the overall plan," he said with a glint in his eye.

"What's that?" I asked.

"My wife is not going to hear of you taking us out to dinner. Among other things, mainly you being our guest, she will argue convincingly, as a doctor too, that going out does not fit properly with an 'unwinding' plan. So, thank you for your generosity but leave the weekend to us. Besides, I'm certain you will be pleased with what she's prepared for supper, not to mention the black forest cheesecake she's made from scratch for dessert."

"Who am I to argue with that kind of logic?" I leaned back in his easy chair, flashing a big smile.

What started on the train as a great conversation and the first steps towards a meaningful friendship, took another leap forward during the weekend. By Sunday night I had grown to admire many more of the facets of this man from Wheatley Hill. Coming from a modest income family, he had worked hard to earn his medical degree. Never forgetting his beginnings, he had kept in his heart the plight of the common man in the healthcare system. He could have chosen private practice but backed up his beliefs by forfeiting a greater income, and chose a career in the less lucrative National Health Service.

I was also struck by his love for the simpler things in life and the contentment he derived from them. Among many things, his love for nature was intoxicating. Our weekend walks around the fields behind his house were filled with discussions on the habits of skylarks, swifts, owls, foxes and many more. I felt myself beginning to breathe again, to take deep breaths, and enjoy the crispness in the air. I felt myself coming back to life. I had grown up playing in the woods, and our jaunts here in Sadberge were bringing back flashbacks of some of my favorite memories.

The stark contrast between these moments of sublime contentment and the bitter battles I faced daily in the highly contentious world of high technology and corporate politics began to weigh heavily on my thoughts. My new friend Edwin had unknowingly brought to my heart the price I had been paying and the struggle I had been avoiding.

Sipping tea in front of their fireplace, I began asking myself what it would take for me to stop the madness. From the day I married my wife, her father and mother had serious concerns on how I, a happy-go-lucky Virginia boy with mediocre grades in college, would be able to support their daughter in the way she was accustomed. I accepted that gauntlet for the challenge it was. I threw myself into my studies, and after receiving my degree, committed myself to succeeding in the corporate world at all cost. I would prove to them their concern was unfounded. By the time I was thirty two, I had been very fortunate to have worked my way into a job which managed one of the largest employment operations in America at the time. My team of thirty one talented people hired eight thousand seven hundred people in two years! Thanks mainly to their superhuman efforts, I got promoted to a Corporate Director level position, managing fifty three Human Resource people covering the United States, Canada, Western Europe, Japan and Australia. At thirty four, I was traveling the world, and in the corporate vernacular, "playing with the big dogs."

However, as I mentioned above, it came with a heavy price. I had felt the pangs of it even before my trip to Sadberge. Sadberge was only the catalyst. All of the perquisites that came with my job, and they were many, only diverted my attention from the real issue at hand: the amount of time I had to spend away from my wife and children. It was draining me, and more importantly, draining them dry. The old memory tapes of proving myself to Ellen's parents just had to stop. By Sunday night, with a real sense of clarity, I resolved to quit my job.

"Are you sure this is what you want to do? Perhaps you should give it some time." Edwin offered in a consultative tone.

"I have given this quite a bit of thought. This weekend has just been a final wonderful "wake up call." Honestly, I can't be a good husband and a good father while working in this kind of a job. That really is the bottom line. No amount of money is worth it to me. I need to call Ellen and let her know my thinking. I know she will be for it."

"What will you do to earn a living? What is your plan?" he said. I could see his part doctor – part good friend "genes" taking hold.

"I think I'm going to step out of the corporate world and become an Executive Recruiter. A real good friend of mine, and former Chief Financial Officer of our computer company, has been asking me to start my own business and work closely with his venture capital firm. It's a bit of a risk, but I know he's someone I can trust."

"Well, the good news is, you do know a little bit about recruiting." Edwin rarely let a moment pass without injecting his dry wit. "And from what I understand, Ellen has more than enough talent to run the books, and keep you squared away."

"Let me tell you, Edwin. No truer words were spoken."

"We're both lucky men. My Kim comes out of the same cut of cloth."

"Think about this. I'll cut my commute from fifty seven miles one way, to working out of our house!" I raised my hands in celebration. "I almost can't imagine getting two and a half hours back out of every day of just being in my car."

"I'm hoping it will give you time to write some letters. I can't wait to hear how this is going to play itself out." He gave me a look of expectation.

"You will. I love to write letters. You may be sorry you made that request. Now, why don't we celebrate over another piece of Kim's cheesecake?"

"I'll say this. Clearly, you have your priorities in order." He got up and started heading for the kitchen.

As we said our goodbyes at the train station, I knew that something special had happened. I didn't know what would materialize or how it would play itself out, but I did know a very unique foundation had been laid.

From these "footings" has come one of the most amazing friendships I have ever known. Together we have walked with each other through trials, tribulations, family crises, births, deaths, job changes, life threatening surgeries, and more. We have entrusted members of our family to each others' care. We have shared our greatest fears, and most thrilling joys. All of this came from an inescapable desire to continue the conversation we began on the train. I am sure today neither one of us thinks that it will ever be finished.

I have always looked at it as a great gift, one with lifelong implications. Most importantly, I have found his deep, abiding faith profoundly stimulating and encouraging. As a writer, our exchanges of ideas and ever expanding personal testimonies have not only wonderfully stretched my understanding of who God is, but also filled my heart with the desire to express these discoveries, these new steps in faith exploration, with words.

PART THREE:
INSPIRATIONS AND
EXPRESSIONS

Poetry

*"A poem…begins as a lump in the throat,
a sense of wrong, a homesickness, a lovesickness…
it finds the thought and the thought finds the words."*

Letters to Louis Untermeyer. January 1, 1916
Robert Frost

Robert Frost was right. I remember the first feelings, those first lumps in my throat, or better said those first thoughts that somehow begged to be written down and captured. They came and went faster than I could handle them. So did the words. Yes, it is as he says, I too found I didn't have to choose them. The feeling would help me write without thinking. It was better that way. The feeling knew what it wanted to say; I would just remember. So let's give three cheers for dear Mr. Frost.

But before "Bobby" takes his congratulatory bow, I think you might want to consider that he didn't lay out the whole story. Let me explain. Yes, the thought finds the words, but the question is why? Why does it seek out the words? What compels the thought to find the words? In my experience the thought is fueled, motivated, and driven by the intensity of remembering. When the current thought stimulates or connects with a past emotion or series of emotions, it automatically initiates a chain reaction. Separately, these emotions often only stir in our subconscious. However, linked together, they become a force to be reckoned with. The unsuspecting current thought is simply the catalyst which ignites this whole chain reaction. The more events and past emotions that are connected, the greater reaction.

I offer this as support for the argument. I happen to look at raindrops on a window. Because I connect rain with a number of emotional events, my mind senses the chain reaction forming and rationalizes that I need more time. Perhaps this is because I wasn't finished dealing with the thought the last time it arose. A moment turns into a few moments and often into minutes. Suddenly I can't stop staring and seem locked in a hypnotic state. Have you ever felt this way? Have you caught yourself staring at something and were not sure why you couldn't stop? The waiting comes to a close when the sometimes convoluted and complex thought connection is made with the past. It is at this moment the thought starts looking for the words. For me, the raindrops on the window start to become manifestations of something more than beads of water. The momentum builds. The thought process having been triggered, begins uncovering words and forcing them out of my subconscious repository into my consciousness. As this all begins to unfold, my imagination picks up the scent and offers its own construct to the fervor. The desire to put pen to paper becomes acute. It becomes acute because you realize that these emotions, almost like wild animals, have been pacing, stirring, waiting for a moment to emerge. Again, it is the linkage with the current event that opens the door. They run out with reckless abandon. Ironic as it may seem, capturing them on paper gives them release. It is as if all they ever wanted was to be vocalized and understood.

What you will find in the following pages, is this cycle occurring over and over again.

Inspiration: Sitting in my '57 Volkswagen, waiting for a light to change. Watching Virginia rain act out its role on my windshield.

A RAINDROP ON A WINDOW

A bead of water
Trickles so slowly
Down a varied course
Straying, sliding, seeking
As if to grow and find
Another of its kind
Yet seeking in so slow a motion,
It is as if some sort of sensitivity
Played upon it;
Seeking stage by stage,
Bead by bead
Until a peak is reached
Then it succumbs,
Awaiting still another day
Another life.

Inspiration: *Searching for a lost grandfather, with a cousin, and a friend on a cold, windy Virginia night.*

"Wind, was that you?"

The clamor of innocent feet
Caroling to the swallowing abyss of darkness,
Stepping forward into the night
Ever moving, always fearing, simply walking
Challenging each corner
Shrouded in darkness and silence,
To have its way with my fear.
Wind, was that you?
Onward, slowly, slowly up the alley
Toward the light,
Eluding the outstretched arms
Of lunging grey shadows
Murmuring death.
Onward, onward, onward
Towards the light.
Wind, was that you?
Tonight, I am filled with fear
Yet hoping your voice
The voice that shares
Implausible stories,
Will come quietly out of the night shadows
To end this nightmare
And the horrible music
That is ringing in my ears.

Inspiration: The funeral of a grandmother. Dealing with the loss; too much pain to cry.

IN MEMORIAM

The hollow sound of steps
Slowly making their way through the church
The church door cracks, almost pleading
Is she gone?
Pounding, sounding
Up the aisle
Echoing onward…is she gone?
The day is dark
The clouds cover the sun
There's rain; it hides the pain
I find I am too numb to cry
My squinted eyes can only ask
Is she gone?

Inspiration: A weariness compounded by a lot of homework and a fatalism born by vivid memories.

LIFE

Learn this,
Do this,
Can't do,
Must do,
Enjoy life,
Too late!
I'm dead.

Inspiration: From the backseat of my mother's car, staring at a sunset while driving on Staples Mill Road.

ODE TO THE SKY

Cold, naked sky
You are the canvass
For the greatest painter of them all.
Think not of Rembrandt, Da Vinci,
Or Michelangelo
For theirs was beauty
Think of the magnificence
Which belongs to only one - the sun.
Crimson, gold, yellow rays,
Among many,
Scattered brilliantly along realm;
Yet ironic though it seems that
A plunging death into the horizon
Brings about such a masterpiece
Upon yourself.
Why must tragedy so often precede greatness?
Some might answer
How can there be true greatness
Without overcoming
Some element of tragedy?
Sky, have honor, for you hold
The answers, and this evening
The artwork of
The greatest painter of them all.

Inspiration: *Driving up Monument Avenue in Richmond, Virginia, about two blocks west of the Maury Monument. I was in the back seat of my father's car, momentarily looking out at a very pretty teenage girl sitting in the back seat of her mother's car.*

LIFE HAS MANY TURNS

My mind out far
I began to see,
A little blue car
On the side of me.

My eyes gained focus,
My heart began to whirl,
I came to notice
A beautiful girl.

I offered a wink,
She returned a smile,
Our hearts were linked
At least for a while.

Alas it happened
When things seemed great
My car turned
And hers went straight!

I lost my chance
There was no time to cry
With a wave and a glance,
I said goodbye.

Inspiration: *A blank cinderblock wall in a quiet high school study hall; a bright afternoon Virginia sun and memories of a brother who brought home every animal in the nearby woods.*

I SAW MORE

I stared at pictures on a wall
That weren't even there;
Yet I saw more than
That wall might ever bear;
Rabbits, snakes, dogs
In flight
Everything I could imagine
From shadows in the light
My hands made up
A thousand things
And some even flew with wings.
It's funny what my wall can be
Whatever my heart can dream
Or my mind can see.

Inspiration: *Walking near Capitol Square in Richmond, staring down at some old brick sidewalks as I made my way. Thinking about the Union and Confederate soldiers who might have stood there or passed this way themselves.*

SIDEWALKS

The sidewalks were made of bricks,
Aged with years of dirt
So stamped into them
They would be dirty forever;
They were filled with cracks in their faces
Likes scars and wrinkles on a man.
I walked on these epics of time
Tombstones to the ground below
And thought of all the people who'll walk
As I, and who will die
Yet the sidewalks will still be there.

Inspiration: *Newly married, we were adjusting to our new baby and a hectic schedule during my junior year at Richmond College. I would attend class in the morning, come home at noon to relieve Ellen. This allowed her time to go off, catch up on some errands and attend afternoon classes at Westhampton College. Both Richmond and Westhampton were part of the University of Richmond. I had a job from 6 p.m. until 10:00 p.m. selling shoes at a nearby Thalhimers Store. From ten until midnight I worked on homework, which I hadn't finished during the day.*

A Day of Us

It's rise and shine at seven
And breakfast in jeans,
You usually eat cereal
And I have the same.

"Don't forget your vitamin,
Don't forget your books –
Goodbye, don't forget, I love you,
Say goodbye to Daddy, Drew."

Oh, I forgot my wallet
And I forgot my keys –
"Do me a favor darling,
Take a morning nap, please."

"Hurray, Daddy's home,
Why are you home so soon?
Look, I have some errands
Watch Drew while I'm gone."

Remember the hour of one o'clock
For then he's off to bed;
Remember the hour of three o'clock
For then he must be fed.

Home again, my darling,
"How's my little one?
O, honey, I'm so happy
We have a little son."

Next we're eating dinner
Which we gobble down,
Oops! It's close to six o'clock
Drew's beginning to frown.

Hurry up and warm the food
He's wanting to be fed,
Bottle next, then we burp,
And off he goes to bed.

It's been a long day honey,
It's time we go to bed –
"What! You are not sleepy?
Is something wrong with your head?"

Now its' midnight,
Homework's written and through
Time to join you darling,
Time to be with you.

It's rise and shine at seven
And breakfast in jeans –
You usually have some cereal
And I have the same.

Inspiration: *Woods for me were always the best playgrounds of them all. As a child they held a wonderful mystique. It was the land of tree forts, hide-and-go seek, Army battles and exploration. Later, as an adult the woods became a place for solitude and reflection. The next two poems were spawned by walks there.*

WHERE I FEEL FREE

I walked into the woods today
And turned myself into a tree
I stood there and watched the world go by-
By my secret place, where I feel free.
I often hide among the leaves
Where no one sees or hears me think
It gives me time to clear my thoughts
It gives me time to find new strength.

A Silence in September

As evening consumes another day
And sunlight melts in distant pine
While breeze blown aspen sway to and fro
And mountains edge a deep blue sky
A silence abounds
Shadows draw nigh.

When all about are fading hues
Soon I see them glisten above
Like fairy dust sprinkled from the Sandman's hand
Faint at first, then sharper still
Thousands and thousands
The heavens they fill.

Alas, I feel an ominous chill
It heralds the start of summer's farewell
Calling to aspen to play out their role
Turning the mountainside from green to gold.
Seasons, they come slowly at first
Then often emerge wonderfully bold.

Inspiration: This next set of poems express the emotions of meeting and falling in love with my soul mate, Ellen.

WITH YOU

It's a little before noon~
I can tell because the sun's
Not quite overhead.
I spent all morning
Walking through the streets,
Talking with people,
Sharing my life,
Absorbing theirs.
This afternoon~
I just want to be with you.

DRIFTING TOGETHER

I'm as far away now
As that stare I see you wearing;
I watch your eyes drifting
And I find myself wanting
To be there drifting with you, peacefully;
Much like I do when I watch
You sleep in the morning.
We've spent the whole day together
Without saying a single word
And it has not mattered;
Our hands, our lips, and our hugs
Have done all the talking.
I know now if I put my head
In your lap
You will smile,
Softly rub my forehead
Until I fall helplessly asleep.
I love days like today.

The Wonderful Wizard of Rain

We're off to see the wizard
The wonderful wizard of rain!
Is that how it goes?
Not hardly;
But that's what we sang as we
Chased thunderstorms through the flowers
Across the valley today.
You said all the daisies were diamonds
And set out to pick everyone.
When I asked you what you were
Going to do with all those diamonds
You said-
"I'm going to buy today and play it again tomorrow."
What a beautiful way to say I love you.
O, how I love the smell of rain.

On a Day like Today

To look at the sun
You'd never think it would stop shining;
Only you could say that
On a day like today;
Rain everywhere and more rain to come.
You'd think we'd prayed for rain
The way we walked barefoot
Through the mud puddles and chased
Popsicle sticks through the swollen gutters.
Barefoot,
Wet bellbottoms,
Two drowned rats,
Smiling, laughing,
Holding hands-
To look at the sun, you'd never think it
Would stop shining.

ALONE AT THE BEACH

Whenever I go to the beach
I love writing my name in the sand.
I can never spell it all
Before it disappears into
The salty foam of a fresh wave.
Sometimes I cross messages
Written by someone else.
Some of the greatest reflections
Ever written
Are resting on beaches
Somewhere between here and Australia.
I can't tell how lonely
These waves today sound
All I can tell you is
I wish you were here.

Inspiration: For six and a half years I was a member of the National Guard. For part of my time, I traveled from Winchester, Virginia to Richmond to attend my once a month drill weekends. I would get up at 4:00 a.m. Saturday morning and return home early Monday morning before heading off to work. Both of the next two poems were written while quietly making my way.

RETURNING HOME

The sky is painted black
And the stars shine on the back of my car.
The telephone poles march by
In line with the sky
And I know that home's not far.

Route Fifty west,
White lines filing one by one;
Pushing through empty streets,
Through towns that softly sleep
One hour past Warrenton.

A slowly brightening sky,
A ground filled with morning dew;
A river nearly still,
Lights from a distant hill
And a journey that's almost through.

I'll be home soon, my darling
I'll be home soon.

Does This Highway Ever End?

Two headlights, an empty road
Singing some song of years gone by
Dreaming things that might have been
Dreaming them over again and again.

Counting the miles as they pass along
Like the white lines down the middle of the road
Road signs hit by my headlights
Slowly pass, and fade into the night.

The tires hum a constant tune
Changing only with the speed of the car
And from my ears it comes and goes
Just like the songs on the radio.

And does this highway ever end
Or does it grow with each day?
Will it lead me safely home
Or will it take me far away?

Inspiration: I was sitting at the dining room table, staring out the window of my dear friend's home in Sadberge, England, a quiet place which has always been a place of rejuvenation for me.

A Wellhouse Window

Each day
Another vestige of spring
Moves closer,
And closer
To the backdoor
Of this Wellhouse.
The trees and the shrubs
Stirred by the warming wind
Are waking
From their long winter's sleep
Stretching their arms
And showing
The first signs of vernal life
With traces of new buds
Coming out
Like painted fingernails
On a young girl's hand.

All of the birds
Are revisiting their former homes
They left in haste
Cruelly evicted
By the cold brutish landlord
Winter.

But now,
As the sun orders,
Temperatures rise
And winter's ownership
Is revoked.
Begrudgingly, he packs and leaves

Releasing his fierce grip
And giving way
To the open hand
Of a new renter
Spring.

Garden doors locked tight
Are reopened
And the new tenants of spring
Begin setting up house
Like relatives or friends reuniting
To share a vacation home.

There is song in the air.
A chorus forms around the birdfeeder.
Blackbirds sing bass,
English Robins blend in baritone,
Meadowlarks chime in with tenor
While Finches and Swifts
Compete for soprano.

Crickets and grasshoppers
Supply the woodwind
While frogs and toads
Boldly bellow
Persistent percussion-
The symphony is glorious!

I find myself
Mesmerized
By the orchestration
And rapt
Daydreaming
Of the terraced garden
That divides the yard
Soon to be filled with
Vivid colors of the newly

Sprouting crocus
And pure white snowdrops
Bursting forth
And defining
A new seasonal palette
On this newly leveled canvas.

Today we are in England,
Northern England
And tomorrow we head for America
I am not longing
For home.
I shall miss this window
In the dining room
And the garden green
Just beyond my touch
But never far, no never far
From my heart.

Inspiration: A walk along a beach in Kauai, watching the waves form and move to the shore. They reminded me of lines of a military band as they pounded their drums and sounded their cymbals. I was amazed at their relentlessness and the power they had to bring things up from the depths of the sea and release them on the beach. I found my thoughts doing the same.

ALWAYS REMEMBERED, ALWAYS ADORED

I walked along the beach today
heard pounding surf upon the shore
my mind let go a thousand thoughts
hidden behind my soul's locked door.
So out they rolled upon the beach
like shells coughed forth from crashing waves
some I'd known for a long, long time
some I met only yesterday.

My mother first came to my mind
recalling how she loved the shore
only got there a very few times
never grieved or wanted more.
She always held a sense of duty
everyone first before herself
lived for family, served her friends
never asked for anything else.

When death came knocking at her door
she held her tongue, all complaints erased
kept her charm and veiled her pain
resolved to die with a sense of grace.

As I watched the waves like regiment lines
march their way from ocean to shore
they played their song for Marguerite McDonough
always remembered, always adored.

Inspiration: I have a good friend named Gwyn. I wanted to give her a gift for her new daughter. I wrote this poem reflecting on my own experiences reading stories to my children.

FROM THE MOMENT I HELD YOU

From the moment I held you
I knew
I would soon cherish the days
When I could sit you in my lap
And watch you point
At all the pretty pictures.

From the moment I held you
I knew
You would have favorite stories
That would make you
Giggle and smile
And you would want me to read them
Over and over again;
And gladly I would.

From the moment I held you
I knew
I couldn't wait to hear
You make the sounds of the animals
Roaring like a lion
Mooing like a cow
Or baa-ing like a baby lamb
As you joyously
Spot them and want me
To know just what they are.
Or the wonderment in your eyes
When you turn the page
And see a butterfly
For the first time.

From the moment I held you
I knew
You would soon read the words
Yourself
That you would master
The stories
They would speak
More to your heart
Than to your eyes.

From the moment I held you
I knew
I wanted to give you the words
As my mother
Gave them to me.
And though you
Will only sit in my lap
For such a short time
May what we share
Be indelibly written
On the pages of our lives
Forever.

Inspiration: My wife has been given, among many, the great gifts of organization and resourcefulness. She continually amazes everyone who crosses her path with these abilities. I was reading a nursery rhyme to one of our children and thought about who could have put Humpty Dumpty back together again.

ODE TO A RESOURCEFUL WIFE

Humpty Dumpty sat on a wall
Humpty Dumpty…
Could have had a chair if he'd only asked Ellen.
She would have found him one,
The right one, at the right cost
With a safety belt and buckle
And all would not have been lost.
If given the time
She would have found a way
To stop his disastrous rhyme
And all the king's horses
And all the king's men
Could have stayed home with their families
And enjoyed the fall…
Weather, that is.

Inspiration: The first tug of the current in a river, wanting to pull my legs downstream.

In the River Again

Oh God,
I am in the river again.
Are you sure this is where
You want me to be?
Don't you understand?
Rivers take you places!
I used to think rivers were for swimming and cooling your feet
But one day while soaking my toes
I noticed
My legs being pulled down the stream
And realized
That every river is being pulled
And water,
Though it may swish in an eddy
Or rest in a pool
Is going somewhere.
It has to.
It needs to fulfill its purpose.
I have always believed you created
Every single person
For a purpose.
Is that why you have drawn me here, Lord?
This whole thing is about a journey
And a purpose... your purpose
Isn't it Lord?
Okay, I am in the river.
Lead on...

Inspiration: *My dear friend Edwin Pugh sent me a book called "Proverbial Philosophy". It was written by Martin Tupper and published in London in 1852. Among the many thoughts and arguments included, there was a poem, "Of To-day", he wanted me to read and then respond in whatever method I would choose. I am sure Edwin wanted me to focus on a verse concerning a staircase where the steps below fell away with every upward step. However, what leapt into my thoughts was another earlier nearby verse, mentioning the pilot of a ship. The line went… "Behold, thou art the pilot of the ship, and owner of that freighted galleon, competent, with all thy weakness, to steer into safety or be lost." The minute I read it, I could see the pictures and feel words begin to bubble in my mind. They consumed my thoughts for days. It took me about two weeks to finalize exactly what I wanted to say.*

THE GOOD SHIP TODAY

The birth of this work was born in your gift,
A challenge from you, words I should sift.
"Of Today", the poem, the ship that would sail;
Thoughts I return, in verse and in tale…

Morning beckons him with dawn's first light,
Deep from the shadows out of the night,
By sending him gulls with songs so clear,
Kittiwakes, Fulmars to sailors are dear.

Command her he must, he shouts to the wind,
Let the forces that play be at it again.
It's up with the sails and anchors aweigh,
Push out from the dock, the good ship Today.

Mind you the bow and off to the stern,
The game's afoot with lesson to learn.
It's ready about, and hard alee,
Out of the harbor toward difficult seas.

Each day is a journey all to its own,
Sometimes as pilot you feel quite alone.
Hand on the wheel, and face to the wind,
Courage to press on comes from within.

Just how do you build that fire below?
How does your soul know not to let go?
What keeps his ship from losing its way?
Mused the lone pilot of good ship Today.

He stared at the compass hours on end,
He stared at the sails pregnant with wind.
He stared at the ocean and crests of the waves,
He wondered what was it that made them behave.

The ocean is vast as big as the sky,
My ship is small, a speck in the eye.
Yet the eye is only a part of the whole,
Could there be more than what I've been told?

And so he labored throughout the day
While steering his course on good ship Today.
Asking himself, just what is it I seek?
Then he noticed his ship had a leak.

Desperately he tried to deal with this spring,
Knowing too well the fate it could bring.
All ships take on water, he knew in his mind,
But leaks like this are deathly unkind.

As he struggled to save his life on the sea,
He asked himself just how could this be?
With all of his might he set out to bail,
"I can't let this happen, I will not fail".

Try though he did, the battle was lost,
Now he would pay a terrible cost.
He fell to his knees to make his amends,
Good-bye to his wife, his family, his friends.

"If only I had just one more day,
I know what I'd do, what I would say.
It's clear to me now, path and the way",
Cried the pilot of good ship Today.

"God I don't know you, I've not even tried
Yet think I've seen you here by my side
Pointing to compass, to wind and sail
Trying to reach me and so to prevail."

"Hear me O Lord, come in to my heart,
I open the door before I must part.
Deal with me now, right here on the sea,
It's all in your hands, so it must be."

No sooner the words had left his mouth,
Then came a ship straight up from the south.
He watched the sloop pull next to his side,
The captain yelled over, "how 'bout a ride?"

So the pilot walked out of Today,
Left some memories, took some away,
Gazed as his ship gave way to the sea,
Began to think of what was to be.

He set a new course, made up his mind,
Bought a new ship, a "three-masted" kind,
Put on a new smile, cast off his sorrow,
Decided he'd name her, the good ship Tomorrow.

Inspiration: *I wanted to give two dear friends, Paul and Sheila Caputo, something from my heart; something that would celebrate how special their love is; something that would reflect on their history and the unmistakable hands that kept bringing them back to each others arms. I interviewed Paul a couple of times, ferreting out moments of their journey; then prayed for the rest.*

On The Eve Of Your Wedding

Three first dates and three first kisses
Making mistakes, weathering storms
Knowing too well within their hearts
Just why this day was…meant to be.

A simple date at Olive Garden
Another date Tobacco's way
Just recovering from former trysts
Not taking life…too seriously.

Love is patient. Love is kind.
It does not envy nor does it boast
It is not rude nor is it proud
Love beckons to love… unselfishly.

Now "Jungle Boy" fell off the vine
And dear Janine was on her way
So movie nights in Powhatan
Let best friends share…quite tenderly.

He almost moved to Illinois
As she came home from Honduras
Both seemed headed in different ways
But not too fast…assuredly.

They found that they both loved to cook
And ever talked of recipes
And built a love on future dreams
Of distant lands…beyond the sea.

A Nags Head night, and love's sweet pact
That they'd hold on as grad school loomed
He watched her leave for Monterey
He knew he'd miss her… passionately.

True love is not irritable
And ne'er rejoices when someone's wrong
It holds out its hand and seeks what's best
Love does not demand…insistently.

Living apart, time took its toll
And doubts arose, so uncontrolled
The hardest thing, is setting free
Your life's true love…willingly.

And thus it seemed, that all was lost
But more than fate was moving now
Within their souls a longing came
She wrote him first…purposefully.

"Can we talk" was all she wrote
Amazed he mused- she must know my mind!
"What's your life like?" is all he asked
Hiding his pain…guardedly.

Now Love rejoices in the truth
It always hopes and always trusts
Bears all things, and believes them true
And ever perseveres…joyously.

She bared her soul, crying aloud
Hearing her tears, he melted inside
After they spoke, to Richmond she flew
Eager to talk… and so was he.

So talk they did for hours on end
Came to a place they'd known from the start
That he loved her and she loved him
It's what really mattered… actually.

Now "milepost ten" is hallowed ground
By wooden band, now diamond ring
And what seemed lost has now been found
True love abounds…gloriously.

So raise your cups, and cherish this
A single thought for all to sift
Love this true is precious indeed
That finds its roots…eternally.

So here's to Sheila and here's to Paul
Friends were they first, now soul mates for life
Ready to share the worst and the best
Thankful this day…was meant to be.

Inspiration: My career has taken me to the ends of the earth, on a wide variety of modes of transportation. The experiences have always been a double edged sword; fascinating in one perspective, seeing something new for the first time; lonely in the other, not being able to share it with my soul mate. I quickly learned there was a finite amount of time I could be away without longing to return to her arms. There were too many days where I was at the mercy of an airplane schedule, a distance to be covered, or a route to be traveled. Too many days the pain was debilitating and accentuated the longing.

O MATE OF MY SOUL

O mate of my soul
As I long for you
The whole of you comes to me
Deeper seeded than memory
More intimate than diary
More feeling than touch
And more fragrant than smell.
I imagine your voice
And I can tell
That every part of me, knows you
Knows you well.
I know that you know things about me
That I am afraid to admit.
I quit wondering how
Resolved
Only to marvel at the insight
True love reveals.
I feel your presence
Whether you are near me or not.
It is as if our souls have found a place
To commune
In a reality far, far more permanent
Than the caring clasp of our hands
Or the tender touch of our lips.
Yet I long for you, long for you
Like a candle longs to be lit

And a beach longs to be hit, and covered
And caressed by the waves.

O mate of my soul
The whole of me
Races to be with you again.

Inspiration: I was talking with a friend who was enrolled in his doctoral program in philosophy. We were discussing a paper he was writing and in making one of his points he used a phrase "Restaurant of Truth". He used it in an allegorical context; however, it put the seed in my mind to speculate on what a real restaurant would look like, who would come, and what would happen.

THE RESTAURANT OF TRUTH

The world has a place, where it feeds every face
the people they come from afar,
I passed by it one night, and noticed its lights,
stopped and got out of my car.

I stood there and looked, at a building that took
a corner lot all to it's own.
'Twas open for food, and I in the mood
sat down at a table alone.

The choices were broad, and I thought it odd
no waiter had come to my booth,
when up came a man, stretching out his hand
saying welcome to the Restaurant of Truth.

I said it's quite funny, I'm sure there are plenty
of reasons why you chose that name
the waiter he said, I'll get you some bread
then come back and try to explain.

My interest it rose, I began to suppose
just what had driven the mind
who thought of the name, and thus had laid claim
to a diner, so different in kind.

The walls they were filled, with writings that chilled
my eyes, they were fixed in a stare
I kept on reading, the verses were leading
a spectrum from hope to despair

I marveled at all I saw on the walls
such thoughts were fervently shared
by travelers whose souls, had come to be bold
and emptied out all that they dared.

The waiter returned, and slowly I learned
the history of what was in view,
he'd published an ad, with all that he had
"Come with one truth you know to be true."

The people they came, they came without shame
their causes on the end of their pen,
they argued and fought, and feelings grew taut
strong wills were not ready to bend.

We'll write it all down, they yelled with a frown
then raise our hands, our votes to cast
and so they did write, long into that night
listing the truths first to the last.

And when they were done, they were sure that one
would hold up to challenge or test
So up on the walls, they stapled them all
to decide which truth would be best.

They went on and on, no truth could hold on,
though some touched the hearts of the crowd
'round this room, came feelings of gloom
on all save one, his head was bowed.

What are you doing, said they who were fuming
your praying is simply absurd
The man raised his head, and softly he said
there's one truth you have not heard.

What are you saying! You can't be relating
to all that's been written or shared
What is it we've missed, some shouted with fists
speak your will, your soul can be bared.

All eyes were on him, their faces were grim
as he stood up to give his reply
the silence was deafening, and many were questioning
which of the truths had passed them by.

And so he began, this simple young man
to share from the depths of his soul
a life full of learning, of seeking and yearning
the one truth that made a man whole.

I've struggled with reason, through each of life's seasons
he said with a smile on his face
I've struggled with feelings, and found myself reeling
when faced with the truth about grace.

I've sometimes deserved the things I have been served
but am thankful I did not pay all
the cost of my actions, or reap the reaction
when the piper came by for a call.

I've seen people die, I have watched them cry
sadly in their great moments of pain
I've seen some survive, so miraculous that I've
been struck by their will to remain.

I have learned that life, with all of it's strife
is as fragile as dew on the rose.
Each day should be treasured, as if it were measured
against a life whose length no one knows.

I've not come to teach, I've not come to preach
but give what I know to be true
If you think about grace, you will come to a place
of not what you believe, but who.

I have long often thought, of the grace that was wrought
on the thief who sinned from his youth
at his moment of death, he took one more breath
and reached out to the Giver of Truth.

Just what did he see, as he hung on that tree
that caused him to seek out His face
he wasn't restrained, he knew what he gained
for he grasped the truth about grace.

Faith is the window. Those that look in know
the offer that God gives to man
His Son paid the cost, come stand at the cross
and embrace the grace of the Lamb.

Before he sat down, his words became drowned
in a fury of shouts from the floor
Don't listen to that, pure faith is a trap
screamed the crowd at the man they abhorred.

If that is his truth, let's put him to use
like the rest of our lists in this hall
So they grabbed the young man, with steel hammers in hand
and nailed him, arms spread to the wall.

The young man he cried, cried out as he died
the mob how they cheered with each scream
Come off of that wall! Give God your last call!
Shout out to that Lamb who redeems.

The laughter was loud, from this arrogant crowd
quite happy were they with their deed
so back to their booths, forgetting their truths
to pack up in order to leave.

Suddenly the nails, that held this young male
gave way to the weight of his load
and off the wall, his body did fall
to the floor where once his blood flowed.

The crowd stood and stared, and no one would dare
to utter what made them afraid
could he be alive, how could he survive
the terrible torture we gave.

The young man began, to move his right hand
and not long was up from the floor
the crowd stood there shocked, and all eyes were locked
on the man whose truth they deplored.

Don't fear, my good friends, it's love not revenge
that has brought me from death back to life
You asked me to share, I shared with much care
I prayed it would end all your strife.

I did not demand, or take a strong stand
that you force my truth in your mind
I offered instead, a truth much like bread
to taste it and see what you find.

Each man must decide, where he will reside
when choices are placed in his way
then he took some bread, he broke it and said
I leave you with something to weigh.

This bread is a staple, it's substance is able
to comfort a man's appetite.
But what fills his soul, and makes a man whole
when he's searching in darkness for light.

Just then a great light, broke in through the night
and took him from out of that place
left there on the floor, some words they were scored
"remember the truth about grace."

Some fell to their knees, while others said please
don't tell me this trick has you fooled
This must be a ruse, don't let it confuse
blind faith has a way to be cruel.

O why can't you see, they said on their knees
the truth that he wants us to find
You're blinded by pride, and never have tried
to listen with more than your mind

The mind is a tool, just don't let it rule
without asking your heart and your soul
united they weave, help, judge and believe
the real truth that makes a man whole.

Let's end with a vote, let's also take note
to return a year from this night
Let's leave it to time, time may change some minds
in a year we may see who is right.

They return every year, they come now with fear
especially if one bows his head
So ends my story, said the waiter before
he asked me if I wanted more bread.

I've eaten my fill, but one question still
lingers in the back of my mind
Where do you stand, you saw the young man
and even the words on the floor?

The waiter he paused, he paused just because
he'd struggled with making his choice
Yet he couldn't disguise, the look in his eyes
his answer did not need his voice.

I feed people bread, the waiter he said
when they come and sit in these booths
and if they should ask, I share to the last
the story of the Restaurant of Truth.

**I form the light and create darkness,
I bring prosperity and create
disaster;
I, the Lord, do all these things.
Isaiah 45:7**

A MORNING MEDITATION

Some mornings,
More than others,
You wake up not taking the sunrise for granted.
You realize the enormous power
Of our sun, 93 million miles away
Boldly pulling itself over your horizon
And with its light
Exposing everything in its path.
And this light wakes up a sleeping world…
Those that fly above it,
Those that walk upon it
Those that crawl or swim and
Those that never see the light but feel its warmth.
Every part of creation reacts.
Some run to the shadows
Some step out further into the light
Some do both because they can't decide
Some think hiding seems more natural.
It is the light that gives
Darkness its definition.
And to think the light …was formed….
And by forming the light, God created darkness.
One begets the other.
God knew that.
He knows the power of light.
He hopes we will understand all this when we peacefully watch a
sunrise.

Prosperity and disaster…
God resides in both.
I never see prosperity as a reward, more a blessing, a gift to be shared
Prosperity brings with it encouragement and joy.
Disaster tests the heart, deepens perspective and too…can bring joy.
Joy? Yes, joy…in the knowledge of not being alone,
In the knowledge of clinging to hope not fear
In the knowledge of eternity and not a moment
In the knowledge of what is important
And what is not.
Prosperity adds to the height of joy
Disaster adds to its depth
And both add to the breadth.
And as life sails into each of these two ports
We gain understanding; a heartfelt understanding
That goes beyond knowledge.
It becomes
A part of our every step, a part of our coming and going.
Perhaps, this is the evolution of when knowledge becomes wisdom.
Prosperity and disaster…
I have learned the reason for these is always in his loving hands
And the fruit from each is sweet…and bittersweet
And both ripen and strengthen the vine.
There is a longing to learn more
And in time there is a trust in Him that allows us
To tell Him, in prosperity and in disaster, how much we love Him,
How much we see His faithfulness
And no matter what tomorrow brings
We are content in the knowledge He is God….and He loves us.

Inspiration: A friend of mine at our church asked me to consider writing a
hymn, utilizing the words "Fully devoted followers of Christ". I
struggled for a long while, though not successfully. I couldn't stop
thinking…what constitutes a follower of Christ? The following
poem is the product of that struggle and the words that did come.
My friend, gifted with graciousness and amazing musical talent,
warmly accepted my efforts and gave them more life in a wonderful
melody.

O WILL YOU BE FAITHFUL?

When God calls you forth, he calls you by name
For he knows who you are, your fears, your pain
And thus stirs your soul, puts resolve in your heart
Then patiently waits for his follower to start.
When God calls you forth, he holds out his hand
And asks you to trust his purpose, his plan
He's given you gifts, for spreading his truth
And now wants to know, will you put them to use?

O will you be faithful? Will you step out?
Forsaking your fear, laying down your doubts
Armed with his Word, assured by his grace
Will you accept the trials you may face?
O will you be faithful? Leave comfort behind?
And risk what you treasure, be totally resigned
That all that you have and all that you are
Are found at his cross, love's truest design.

When God calls his church, it's planters he needs
Who'll take the Good News and scatter its seeds
With love and mercy to neighbors and friends
To strangers and enemies, his love knows no end.
When God calls our church, he calls us by name
For he hears our worship, our prayers, refrains
He urges us on to march forward in faith
Teaching us always, in his hands we are safe.

O will we be faithful? Will we step out?
Forsaking our fears, laying down our doubts
Armed with his Word, assured by his grace
Will we accept the trials we may face?
O will we be faithful? Leave comfort behind?
And risk what we treasure, be totally resigned
That all that we have and all that we are
Are found at his cross, love's truest design.

Inspiration: *My dear friend Edwin Pugh introduced us to St. Abbs, Scotland. The quiet walks we had walking the cliffs, marveling at the migratory birds, the sound of the sea crashing against the shoreline, and the picturesque little fishing village whose harbor was nestled in behind concrete sea walls, left an enchanting painting and memorable concert for our souls.*

PERHAPS TODAY

Perhaps today,
If I could play…
I would sit on a rock
Overlooking Horse Castle Bay
Watching a thousand waves finally come home
From their journey across the sea
Each one greeted by a colony of gulls
Whose nests line the cliffs
Like bleacher seats in a coliseum.
The warm cup of tea in my hands
Would feel as good as it tastes
And I would find myself
Wanting to sit there all day.

There is something soothing about the sea
An ever present constancy,
An endless powerful rhythm
Striking and playing the chords of my soul
And every part of my being
Longs for the feeling
Of hearing again and again this rolling lullaby
And I
Find myself
Wanting to sit there for more than a day.

Perhaps tomorrow,
If we could play…
I would take you with me
Past Nunnery Point

To gaze at the harbor
Beyond Horse Castle Bay
And share the melodies
Of day-long concerts
Sung by Seagulls, Gannets, Puffins and thrashing sea
And then sit quietly
While our hearts applaud.

Inspiration: *I began picturing in my mind two men meeting by chance at a river's edge. One has found hope and is purposely waiting to share; the other has none, is wandering and is desperate enough to listen. How would they interact and leave this fortuitous encounter? The two men, each in their own right, are an amalgamation of some people I have met and known well. Lastly, and specifically to this issue of hope, I have never been able to let go the words from Dante's Inferno: "All hope abandon, ye who enter here."*

I Met A Man By The River's Edge

I met a man by the river's edge
Wand' ring my way down a path to the sea
He sat perched on a rock just staring
Reflecting,
When I came by, he turned to look at me.

He had the face of a peaceful man
But there was something more I found unique
I am not sure why I was drawn by his eyes
Then surprised,
When calmly he asked, "What do you seek?"

"I am wandering my way to the sea
Enjoying the colors before they fall
Like the leaves in this slow river's flow
They go,
It's a journey, a season, that's all."

"But what do you seek?" he firmly asked
Not leaving his question unanswered
"The leaves fall without choice
Or voice,
Their purpose will not be remembered."

"I'm not seeking anything", I quickly replied
Recoiling from his brash intrusion
"Perhaps in the end we are like the leaves,"
I seethed
With his obvious annoying conclusion.

"We are like the leaves," he nodded his head
"For truly we live and one day shall die
But surely we are more than the leaves
I believe,
There's more to this life and reasons why."

With all of my might I wanted to leave
Avoiding this challenging chatter
But with reason I stubbornly stayed
Delayed,
To deal with the point of this matter.

Off went my pack and off went my boots
My sore feet I eased in the river
Then slowly turned stared back at the man
To plan,
To cope with his questions and answers.

"What do you seek?" he came back again
Quite like a clock that strikes on the hour
"I seek relief", I coldly replied
To hide,
My thoughts which he seemed to devour.

"What kind of relief?" he calmly replied
Waiting for me to serve up my case
Thousands of answers ran to my lips
But slipped
Back from my tongue as dread took their place.

I wanted to speak but gave no reply
Stared at the river and sky deep blue
I watched the brown leaves running away
In dismay,
I knew I was running away too.

All that I thought were life's long rewards
I fervently chased with all of my might
I ran like the wind, I scaled every hill
Filled,
With achievement both morning and night.

There wasn't a tiger I didn't hunt
There wasn't an ocean I didn't sail
There wasn't a discord I couldn't rhyme
Or find,
A solution that just wouldn't fail.

The harder I pushed, the more that I won
The more that I won, the more that I wanted
There built up in me an insatiable thirst
A curse,
For those who approach life undaunted.

Yet pity obsession at the end of the day
When victories grow cold and trophies colder
Regrets stand tall like indomitable foes,
And throw
Real doubts on this battle worn soldier.

If aging is a furnace then time is its fire
Some lessons I've learned have not been kind
Possessions are logs that glow for a season,
With reason,
Their Memories which fade from the hearths of our minds.

"I'm weary", I sighed. "When does this end?
For nothing I've chased has led me to peace
I war with myself morning and night,
I fight
Hard with my choices, I want this to cease."

Mistakes of the past echo like the waves
Resounding on beaches, memories replayed
I knew that he heard them on the shores of my mind
And finds
I'm hiding behind a smile that's afraid.

"It's not in things," thoughtfully he said
"But you know that, that's not why you're here
There's more on your face than what you are saying,
Portraying,
You're not searching, it is wrestling I hear."

I took a deep breath and froze in place
How could he know what was deep in my soul?
Who is this man who breaks through defenses
And senses
The pain in my heart, and worse its toll.

I decided to share from my wrestling mind
What kept me troubled and wouldn't let loose
Slowly it spilled from laboring thoughts
What I ought
To have said when he first asked for truth.

"I did not come here to see the leaves
I came here because I'm falling myself
Struggling with seasons that rapidly change
What remains
True in this life? On that, let us delve."

"Are we just leaves of another season?
Born for a moment in a family tree
Destined to fall when our winter comes
I'm numb…
From asking myself, what matters to me?"

"Never in my life have I felt so lost
Good friends move away and parent's die
Children grow up, the years roll by fast
What lasts
At all in this world?" I started to cry.

The well of my soul let go of my tears
Out of my eyes, they burned down my cheeks
Like Lemmings they ran and leapt from my chin
"In the end"…
I said, "I am lost with nothing to seek."

Slowly the man got up from his perch
Brushed off his jeans and stood up straight
"I know how you feel. I've stood there too
Like you
I was lost, distraught and about to break."

"I craved a time when new days were new
Where fresh starts were born with morning's first light
Where harbors held ships and nothing more
And doors,
Begged to be closed, things were made right."

"I longed for a chance to bury my past
Finally let go of a thousand regrets
To be like these trees…let go of their leaves
Be relieved
To finally see that this sun had set."

"Like you I came to this river's edge
And saw a man sitting all alone
And he looked at me like none before
He explored
The struggles my face must have shown."

"He had a gift like none I had known
He saw past my words and into my soul
He questioned me like I challenged you
And knew
Just what to ask not leaving his goal."

"His face was a light much like a flame
I felt like a moth unable to flee
His words were gentle yet sure to their mark
In my heart
I wondered…why is he talking with me?"

"Quickly I came like you to the end
Hollow inside with no one to blame
Finally he told me why he was there
He shared
The purpose he found now let me explain."

"Thirst", he said, "is a challenging thought.
What quenches it is more complex indeed
Let's look at water" he motioned to me
So we
Stood in the river, I was intrigued.

"Thirst has two suitors, body and soul
Water quenches the first but will not the last
Ignore your soul, and let it grow dry
You will die
Much like these leaves we see tumbling past."

"When your mouth is parched, you know what you need"
He scooped up water in the palms of his hands
"Simple, sufficient, clearly defined
You find
That this is the relief your body demands."

"But think carefully my friend, what sates the soul?
What will suffice its need or its cry?
Where is the well that relieves its despair?"
He stared
At the water with peace in his eyes.

"What fills a man's soul are words of truth
Generative, profound, transcending time
Always alive, unchanging, a spring
Ever giving
Life to the lost and sight to the blind."

"The quest of this life it is to find what they are
Who is their source? From where do they hail?
Your soul regards them the ultimate prize
And cries
'Immutable truth is a Holy Grail'!"

In the river we stood face to face
Assuredly I knew this wasn't by chance
For all that he'd done was truly sublime
My mind
Started racing, the water it danced.

I knew we had reached the moment of truth
I would find out why we were here
He pulled from his coat a worn brown book
He looked
Humbly at me disarming my fears.

"I offer to you what he gave to me
Words I found living like no other truth
Words of hope, forever resolute
Suitable,
Ebullient, they will never let loose."

"You came to see leaves. Read about trees
Whose leaves never wither nor do they die
Planted by streams they know why they're blessed
They rest
Near the water. Dare ask yourself why."

Never had I seen a face so intent
His fervor the sun, his conviction its heat
Words from his heart so tenderly shared
Declared
With a purpose, his message replete.

For a moment I thought what would I do?
I reached for his book, what could I lose?
I would read fast. How hard could it be?
For he
Spoke to my soul. How could I refuse?

"I leave you with this, he said with a smile
"The same request that that was given to me
Bring back this book six months from today
Relay
What you find, I will wait by the trees."

I waved as I left with book in hand
Wondering if I would ever come back
Wondering if I had been in a dream
It seemed
Overwhelming. I was sure about that.

Springtime is lovely, the leaves how they're born
They break through the buds being fed by the rain
I notice them now as I sit by the trees
A breeze
Blows by softly, its whisper remains.

I have in my hands a worn brown book
I treasure it now like nothing I've known
Yet I know too I must give it away
I pray
For such wisdom as I wait here alone.

I didn't wait long when my brother appeared
Then a sister, her husband and son
Where have you been we've been looking for you?
I knew
Right away what task must be done.

Sometimes it's family, sometimes it's not
It isn't by choice; that is quite clear
Seeds are the issue, the reaping is his
It is
Through his strength that we conquer our fear.

And so I sit by this river's edge
Profoundly grateful, often to tears
Committed to share what was shared with me
Gently
With purpose, with whomever will hear.

Inspiration: *Experiencing a memorable week in Ecuador; listening to the haunting music of a Christian ensemble; observing and absorbing the beauty of creation in the surrounding countryside; meeting and praying with a humble man whose persistence in serving God was captivating and inspiring; realizing the powerful impact of the Living Word on accepting hearts, this psalm came to my heart.*

An Ecuadorian Psalm

There is a rhythm in the mountains of Ecuador
It moves to the sound of the windpipe, the guitar and the drum
And everyone who hears it
Cannot help but respond to the haunting melody
That resonates within their soul.
It is not the cry of Cotopaxi
Mighty mountain, resting giant;
It is not the cry of the eucalyptus,
The blooming century plant,
Nor any flora or fauna
Which so beautifully grace the countryside.
It is not the ancestral spirit of the Incas
Courageous yet conquered people.
It is the call of the Creator
Who sets the moon in the lavender sky
And surrounds it with angel winged clouds
And the shimmering stars of the Southern Cross.
It is the call of our Creator
Who through his amazing love
Sent his only Son
With his tender, tender heart
To the cross to die…and to live!
His heart, the source, beats out
A message like no other message
For it was beating in the beginning
And it will beat forever
For everyone who will hear and believe
The rhythm flowing from the living words
Given from the Creator himself

The almighty Creator
Creator of all people
Creator of Jaime Lomas
And every faithful servant
Who willingly and joyfully risk their lives
To carry the message to those in search of truth
And to those who are waiting to understand
Its awesome nature
Already pulsating within them.
It is for the glory of the Creator
That we breathe every day
Sensing his presence in our every step
Beholding his profound wisdom…
In the constant overwhelming rhythm
That makes its way to the four corners of the earth
And moves in the mountains of Ecuador.

FINAL THOUGHTS

This journey began with the simple goal of sharing some poems and their inspirations. That goal seemed straightforward enough until I began realizing what else came into play, specifically the forces that led me to put words on a piece of paper. Once that happened, I couldn't resist trying to explain it. If I have been able to shed some insight into what I think goes into that creative process, then this effort has achieved part of its purpose.

Writing is the evidence of what is echoing in the mind. I think every writer shares his or her thoughts with the hope that they will find meaning and encouragement for someone. It is a heartwarming validation when you hear what you have struggled to capture in words, is received with the same level of feeling and purpose with which it was conceived.

As for other intentions, I hope that it has been self evident from the beginning. I wanted to share a journey where the turning pages were more than a rambling story. Each page was a step in an ongoing process that helped to define what truly was at the heart of the matter.

For me that definition began to crystallize into one word: Hope. I realized along the way that the fatalism that I had come to embrace, that "O well, such is life" and "What does it matter in the long run, everybody's got to die sometime" type of attitude, was only a set of coping mechanism walls that I had developed to disguise what was really churning in my soul. For the longest time I was content to let it be the right construct, for it projected the resilient cavalier front I wanted and deflected any suspicion that I was struggling. Yet something was wrong. I was hurting inside and the energy it took to placate my internal "Civil War" grew daily.

The whole issue centered on hope. I just couldn't endure what fatalism had to offer. There was simply no regenerative value in it and moreover, every day I felt it sucking the life out of my soul. I needed hope; not just any hope but one that could withstand whatever life threw at it. In addition to its indestructibility, I needed one that never missed offering a saving hand on a discouraging day.

One thing was painfully clear. I didn't have that kind of hope. In fact, what I had was no hope at all. Everything that I assumed was a symbol of permanence began one by one to fail, crumble and fade away. When the last stronghold, the one that I treasured most in life, showed signs of buckling, I became as desperate and lost as I had ever been.

Abraham Lincoln once said, "I have been driven many times to my knees with the overwhelming conviction that I had nowhere else to go." I have kept this quote in my wallet for the last twenty nine years, moved by its poignancy, amazed with its apt description of my own journey, and mesmerized with its profound wisdom.

For it was there on my knees that I discovered the greatest lesson of my life. The same almighty one and only holy God, who by his very word created the heavens, setting the stars and galaxies in their places and brought forth the earth with all its intricate interwoven majesties, is the same tender compassionate God who hears the cry of the brokenhearted, saves those who are crushed in spirit, brings the dead back to life, and patiently and graciously opens the eyes of those who seek him, to the greatest hope ever known.

I owe my life to this hope and the most amazing love on which it is based.

So I come to the end of this book. If Oliver Wendall Holmes, Jr. is correct that each man should share his passion lest he be judged not to have lived, then I hope the reader will accept these pages with the sincerity that they have been offered.

About the Author

Although a native of Richmond, Virginia, he has lived the greater part of his life in Colorado. He is married with two children, and three grandchildren. His mother and father both came from large families. His mother, one of eleven siblings, came from an Irish Catholic family. His father, one of eight siblings, came from an Italian family. Growing up with these two very different cultural styles, provided an abundance of life forming memories. As distinctive as they were, both families shared certain things in common. They both loved to come together for meals and parties no matter the circumstance or day of the week. Each also loved to retell the stories of family experiences and revisit the emotions, both laughter and tears, that came with them. It was as if they knew intuitively the role they played in strengthening their very unique family relationships. The author grew up loving those stories and the directions they laid for his life.

He has spent most of his career in the field of Human Resources, currently working as a Human Resources executive for a biotechnology company in the Seattle, Washington area and spends some time consulting for companies in Minneapolis and Denver. Throughout his career, he has interviewed thousands of people from all over the world and even today continues to spend much of his time listening to the stories which bind people to a course in life or to a dream they hope to achieve.

A love for stories, a desire to express emotions and a delight in creating word pictures, has served as the driving force for his writing.

www.ingramcontent.com/pod-product-compliance
Lightning Source LLC
Chambersburg PA
CBHW061251280526
45784CB00002B/720